GUIDE TO
JAMAICA

including HAITI

IS THIS BOOK OUT OF DATE?

In today's world, things change so rapidly that it's impossible for one person to keep up with everything happening in any one place. This is particularly true of the Caribbean. Travel books are like automobiles: they require frequent fine tuning to stay in shape. Help us keep this book in shape! We need input from our readers so that we can continue to provide the best, most current information available. Please write to let us know of any new information, inaccuracies, or misleading information. Keep notes in the margins of this book — notes made on the spot are always more accurate than those recorded later. Send us your book after your trip, and we'll replace it with a fresh copy. We especially appreciate letters from female travelers, visiting expatriates, local residents, and hikers and outdoors enthusiasts. We'd also like to hear from hotel owners and individuals wishing to accommodate visitors from abroad. If you take a photograph during your trip which you feel might be appropriate for a future edition, please send it to us. Send only good Kodak slide duplicates or glossy black-and-white prints. If we use your photo, you'll be mentioned in the photo credits and receive a free copy of the book. Moon Publications will own the rights to all materials submitted. The publisher bears no responsibility for materials submitted unsolicited, and cannot return any materials without a self-addressed, stamped envelope. Although we try to make our maps as accurate as possible, errors do occur. If you have any suggestions for improvement or places that should have been included, please write to us. Address your letters to:

Harry S. Pariser
Moon Publications
Box 1696
Chico CA 95927

GUIDE TO JAMAICA

including HAITI

HARRY S. PARISER

PUBLICATIONS

Please send all comments, corrections, additions, amendments and critiques to:

**HARRY PARISER
MOON PUBLICATIONS
P.O. Box 1696
Chico, CA 95927, USA**

GUIDE TO JAMAICA

Published by
Moon Publications
P.O. Box 1696
Chico, California 95927, USA
tel. (916) 345-5473/5413

Printed by
Colorcraft Ltd., Hong Kong

All Rights Reserved Hong Kong 1986 Harry S. Pariser

Library of Congress Cataloging in Publication Data

Pariser, Harry S., 1954-
  Guide to Jamaica, including Haiti.

  Bibliography: p. 161
  Includes index.
  1. Jamaica—Description and travel—1981— -Guide
-books. 2. Haiti—Description and travel—1981—
—Guide-books. I. Title.
  F1869.P37 1985   917.292'046   85-19048
ISBN 0-9603322-8-6

*Dedicated to the ebullient spirits of
John Coltrane, Robert Nesta Marley, and Fela Kuti:
three musicians whose compositions have bridged
the gap between Africa and the Americas,
and in so doing, have changed the face of music
forever.*

ACKNOWLEDGEMENTS

Thanks go out to the following individuals who helped with the production of this book. **MOON STAFF:** Deke Castleman and Mark Morris for their thorough editing; Asha, Louise Foote, Kirk Tozer, and William Beach for their patient and painstaking work on the maps; publisher Bill Dalton for his advice and work on the dummying; Dave Hurst for his work on the dummy, layout, camera work, cover, etc.; and to Moon writers Dave Stanley and Peter Harper for their advice. **OTHERS:** Hisashi Motegi, Andy of Lloyd Parkes and We the People for their information on Kingston; Tim Stuart; the James family of Discovery Bay; Peter Bentley; *Exploring Jamaica* co-author Phillip Wright for his extremely helpful comments on my rough draft; John Blackwood for his suggestions and criticism of my Introduction; *San Francisco Bay Guardian* reggae reviewer Bruce Dancis, and Santa Fe reggae reviewer and concert promoter Jack Kolkmeyer for their advice on my reggae section; David Minor for his helpful comments on the Rastafarian section; my mother Trudi for her advice and support; magazine publisher Ron Lippert for his companionship, encouragement, and example of diligence in the face of adversity; Jeffrey Hadley Louden, Nancy Kaufman, Mary Lou "Fluffy" Manning, and "El Nino" Ramsay for putting up with living with me — to various extents and durations — during the hair-pulling period while this manuscript was being forged; the 21 Hayes and 5 Fulton buses who, along with San Francisco's Tenderloin district, served to remind me that America, too, is very much a Third World country; to the *San Francisco Chronicle* whose humorous (albeit unintentionally) editorial pages energized my mornings; to San Francisco Mayor Diane Feinstein and President Ronaldo "Grenada" Reagan whose gaffes abroad and poor policy planning made it clear why more and better travel guides are necessary; and, finally, to the Art Ensemble of Chicago, Don Cherry, Ornette Coleman, and World Saxophone Quartet, whose performances, live and on vinyl, helped keep this Urban Bushman safe, sound, and writing.

black and white photo credits: Harry S. Pariser: p. 28, 32, 38, 40, 42, 50, 55, 77, 81, 83, 86, 88, 91, 101, 103, 106, 108, 114, 123, 125. "Parade Square" by Sidney McClaren (p. 8) and "Revivalism" by Kapo (p. 36) included courtesy of The National Gallery, Kingston. Roy (Johnny) O'Brien, Jamaica Tourist Board: p. 11, 52, 67, 73, 98, 124. Norman D. Hamilton, Jamaica Tourist Board: p. 93. Granville Allen, Jamaica Tourist Board: p. 87. Jamaica Tourist Board: p. 51, 97, 111. Schanachie Records: p. 46-47; "Bunny Wailer" shot by Kate Simon, "Mutabaruka" by Anthony Brennan, "Yellowman" by Sara Rios. Jamaica Information Service: p. 20, 21, 25. C.J. Marrow: p. 137, 138, 139, 143, 149, 150. David: p. 144. ***line illustrations:*** Hopie Windle: p. 14, 19, 30, 57, 126, 158. Jamaica Information Service: p. 39, 69, 90. Louise Foote: p. 127, 145, 147, 155. Harry S. Pariser: p. 140. Drawing on page 115 copyright Pamela Gosner, from *Caribbean Georgian* 1982, Three Continents Press, Washington, D.C. ***color photos:*** Harry S. Pariser, Haitian National Office of Tourism, C.J. Marrow.

about the cover: The front cover photo is of San San beach, Port Antonio, Jamaica while the back is of the Blue Hole nearby. Both were shot by the author using a Konica FC camera with 55mm, f1.4 lens and Kodak KR-36 color slide film.

CONTENTS

JAMAICA

LIST OF MAPS

INTRODUCTION

No other island in the Caribbean conjures up such evocative images as Jamaica. The island's name comes from the Arawak Indian name, *Xaymaca,* which means "Land of Wood and Water." Although best known for reefer and reggae, Jamaica has much more to offer: white sandy beaches framed by the turquoise ocean, the cool and misty heights of the Blue Mountains, the unique historical atmosphere of Spanish Town and Port Royal, the peaceful tranquility of Port Antonio. You'll find plenty to see and do here, a tantalizing variety of food and fruits to sample, lush and varied vegetation to enjoy, and fascinating people to meet.

THE PHYSICAL SETTING

THE LAND

the big picture: The islands of the Caribbean extend in a 4,500-km arc from the western tip of Cuba to the small Dutch island of Aruba. The region is sometimes extended to include the Central and S. American countries of Belize (the former colony of British Honduras), the Yucatan, Surinam, Guiana, and Guyana. The islands of Jamaica, Hispaniola, Puerto Rico, and the U.S. and British Virgin Islands, along with Cuba, the Cayman, Turk, and Caicos islands form the Greater Antilles. The name derives from early geographers, who gave the name "Antilia" to hypothetical islands thought to lie beyond the no less legendary "Atlantides." In general, the land is steep and volcanic in origin: chains of mountains run across Jamaica, Cuba, Hispaniola, and Puerto Rico, and hills rise abruptly from the sea along most of the Virgin Islands.

Jamaica: Third largest island in the Greater Antilles, Jamaica covers 11,420 sq km (4,411 sq miles). Although only

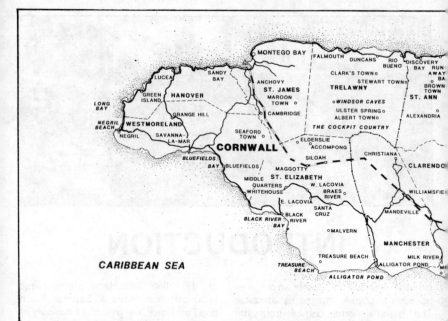

about the size of Connecticut or half the size of Wales, this island encompasses a breathtaking variety of terrain. Mostly rugged and mountainous, nearly half the country is 3,000 m (1,000 ft.) or more above sea level. An enormous mass of limestone comprises two-thirds of the land's surface. For much of its 235-km (146 mile) length, mountains in the highlands run across an E-W axis, reaching over 2,428 m (7,400 ft.) in the east. Secondary ridges and spurs gradually trail off to the narrow stretch of coast below. Jamaica was born 140 million years ago, give or take a millennium, when volcanic mountains thrust upward from the floor of the N. Caribbean. The mountains uplifted limestone formed by the accumulation of eons of dead marinelife. About 100 million years later, the mass submerged. When the East Pacific and Caribbean plates separated some 25 million years later, the

stresses created major structures like the Blue Mountains and faults like the 8,120-m-deep (24,750−ft.) Cayman Trough W of Jamaica. During this period, the East Caribbean plate slid under the North American plate, forcing the volcanic material back up to sea level. As it settled, the island shattered like a three-dimensional jigsaw puzzle. A process known as "Karstification" (water dissolving limestone) produced the pits and grottos of Cockpit Country (see "Cockpit Country" under "South and West Jamaica"). This tropical weathering had the added effect of producing non-soluble mineral deposits of *terra rossa* soils. Dark red in color, they contained concentrations of aluminum hydroxide, popularly known as bauxite. This mineral, millions of years later, was to become the island's major export. The Blue Mountains, which cover the east-central area of the country, are the major range. On both

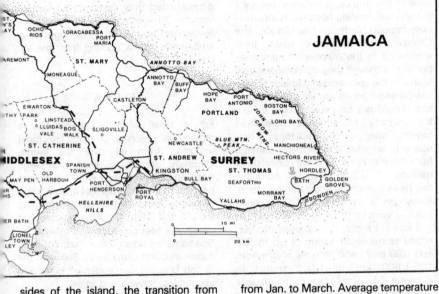

Map labels: ST. N'S AY, OCHO RIOS, ORACABESSA, PORT MARIA, AREMONT, ST. MARY, MONEAGUE, ANNOTTO BAY, ANNOTTO BAY, BUFF BAY, HOPE BAY, PORT ANTONIO, BOSTON BAY, LONG BAY, EWARTON, THY PARK, LINSTEAD, LLUIDAS VALE, BOG WALK, SLIGOVILLE, CASTLETON, PORTLAND, JOHN CROW MTNS., NEWCASTLE, BLUE MTN. PEAK, BLUE MTN. MTNS., MANCHIONEAL, HECTORS RIVER, ST. CATHERINE, SPANISH TOWN, ST. ANDREW, SURREY, KINGSTON, ST. THOMAS, HORDLEY, MIDDLESEX, OLD HARBOUH, MAY PEN, PORT HENDERSON, PORT ROYAL, BULL BAY, SEAFORTH, BATH, GOLDEN GROVE, MORRANT BAY, BOWDEN, YALLAHS, HELLSHIRE HILLS, ER BATH, LIONEL TOWN LEY

0 10 mi
0 20 km

sides of the island, the transition from mountains to sea is abrupt. The coastal plains are broader along the S side than in the north. The most extensive coastal plains run along the Liguanea Plain (largely squatted by Kingston) to the plains of St. Catherine and Clarendon and on to the W coast plains of St. Elizabeth and Westmoreland. Although there are more than 120 rivers, none is very impressive. Hector's River runs underground for five to six km of its course; the Rio Cobre forms a deep gorge at Bog Walk.

CLIMATE

Close to ideal. The warm season is the *only* season in Jamaica. Although up to 508 cm (200 in.) of rain fall each year in parts of St. Thomas and Portland parishes, the average yearly rainfall is 195 cm (77 in.), with March and Oct. being the rainiest months. Main dry period is from Jan. to March. Average temperature is 80 degrees. Kingston averages 86.7 degrees F high and 69.1 degrees F low in Jan. and 90.7 degrees F high and 75.1 degrees F low in July. Temperatures may be 10 to 20 degrees cooler inland. The summits of the Grand Ridge of the Blue Mountains are infrequently touched by frost during the winter months. Cloudy, cool, and damp weather may occasionally occur during the winter when "northers" arrive. Humidity tends to be high: Montego Bay may have 71-77 percent humidity; Kingston ranges from 63 percent in Feb. to 75 percent in October. But the winds really save this island. The "Doctor Breeze," a cool trade wind, prevails during the day, while the "Undertaker's Breeze" sweeps down from the mountains at night. Their combined effect is to make what would otherwise be an unbearably hot and humid environment not only tolerable but actually pleasant to live in.

hurricanes: Cast in a starring role as the bane of the tropics, hurricanes represent the one outstanding negative in an otherwise impeccably hospitable climate. The Caribbean as a whole ranks third worldwide in the number of hurricanes per year, although they are comparatively scarce in the area around Jamaica. These low-pressure zones are serious business and should not be taken lightly. Where the majority of structures are held together only by nails and rope, a hurricane is no joke, and property damage from them may run into the hundreds of millions of U.S. dollars. A hurricane begins as a relatively small tropical storm, known as a cyclone, when its winds reach a velocity of 62 kph (39 mph). At 118 kph (74 mph), it is upgraded to hurricane status, with winds of up to 320 kph (200 mph) and ranging in size from 100-1,600 km (60-1,000 miles) in diameter. A small hurricane releases energy equivalent to the explosions of six atomic bombs per second. Hurricanes may be compared to enormous hovering engines that use the moist air and water of the tropics as fuel, carried hither and thither by prevailing air currents, generally eastern trade winds which intensify as they move across warm ocean waters. When cool, drier air infiltrates it as it heads N, the hurricane begins to die, cut off from the life-sustaining ocean currents that have nourished it from infancy. Routes and patterns are unpredictable. As for their frequency: "June—too soon; July—stand by; August—it must; September—remember." So goes the old rhyme. Unfortunately, hurricanes are not confined to July and August. In Oct. 1954, a hurricane devastated Jamaica and Haiti. Hurricanes forming in Aug. and Sept. typically last for two weeks while those that form in June, July, Oct., and Nov. (many of which originate in the Caribbean and the Gulf of Mexico), generally last only seven days. Approximately 70 percent of all hurricanes (known as Cabo Verde types) originate as embryonic storms coming from the W. coast of Africa.

FLORA

For a small island, Jamaica has a remarkable diversity of plant life, most imported from all over the world. Originally densely covered with large trees, the island lacked what have since become the most famous of its fruit trees, flowering shrubs, and plants. Arriving around the 10th C., Arawaks brought cassava, sweet potatoes, and maize. The Spaniards introduced bananas, coconut, sugarcane, and citrus fruits. Still later, the British brought a number of fruits and vegetables, flowers and trees.

trees: Over a 400-year period, Jamaica has been gradually deforested. Once regarded as the world's finest, West Indian mahogany was a major export during the 18th C., used in high-quality English furniture like Chippendale and Sheraton. Today, however, wood is imported from Honduras because the native Jamaican species is so hard to come by. *Mahoe,* the national tree of Jamaica, flourishes in moist forest glades. The rather small *lignum vitae* bears the national flower. Its name ("wood of life") refers to the medicinal qualities attributed to the tree's resinous gum. Logwood, a native of Central America, is used to produce black and gray dyes. Jamaicans have long believed that *duppies* (ghosts) reside in the spreading branches of the *ceiba* or cotton tree. This enormous tree may live for 300 years or more. The aromatic native pimento tree produces a

Castleton Botanic Gardens, St. Andrew's Parish

substance internationally known as allspice, because its taste is said to resemble that of cinnamon, cloves, and nutmeg combined. The useful ackee and breadfruit trees, with their edible fruits, were introduced by Captain Bligh in 1779 and 1783, respectively. Many other trees are also imports: the mango and tamarind came from India, the almond from Malaya, the casuarina from Australia, and the guango from S. America. "Macca fat" and "prickly pole" are native island palms; the royal palm is a Cuban import. The coconut palm, thought to have come from Malaya, reached Jamaica during the Spanish era. Other trees include the fiddlewood, satinwood, rosewood, West Indian cedar, ebony, Spanish elm, and the tulip tree.

others: Five hundred species of ferns, 80 species of wild pines, and at least 200 species of orchids thrive on Jamaica. Parasitic plants include several varieties of mistletoe and the dodder or "love bush." In the drier areas of S. Jamaica are numerous types of cactus, including the phallic dildo cactus and the prickly pear; several varieties of climbing cactus have night-blooming flowers. Most grasses have been introduced from abroad. Guinea and *pangola* grasses, both used for fodder, came from Africa, while molasses or Wynne grass, which has proliferated in the open areas of the Blue Mountains, was introduced by a Jamaican, Mr. Wynne. The great bamboo is a native of China. The native climbing bamboo, found in the Blue Mountains, has a 32-year life cycle. With pods reaching two to three ft. in length, the *cacoon,* a giant pea vine which grows along rivers, has been known to cover two acres.

FAUNA

Like the flora, most of Jamaica's mammals have been imported. A notable exception is the coney, a large rodent which superficially resembles a brown guinea pig. Once extremely abundant and considered a delicacy by the Arawak Indians, today it's found only in the Jim Crow Mountains of N.E. Jamaica. Its cousin, the rat, reached Jamaica as a stowaway aboard the earliest arriving vessels. Nineteenth C. plantation owners imported mongooses from India, hoping to eradicate the rats. At first the population declined. Then the mongooses learned to climb trees, and their culinary tastes began widening to include birds and lizards. The mongooses became so plentiful that they too became pests, and a commission was formed to exterminate them. Wild pigs roam the mountains. Bats—known as "rat-bats" locally in order to distinguish them from butterflies and moths—come in 25 varieties. Most feed on fruit or insects. With the exception of certain island politicians, vampire bats are unknown here.

birdlife: Jamaica has 25 indigenous species of birds. The doctor bird (or streamtail hummingbird), national bird of Jamaica, is found all over the island. The male's iridescent green breast and scissor-like, elongated tail make it easy to identify; the female lacks these characteristics. The name comes from its practice of puncturing the base or sides of flowers with its bill to draw out the pollen, an act which resembles the 17th C. doctor poking around with his lancet. An iridescent rainbow is revealed each time the mango hummingbird takes flight. The vervain or bee hummingbird, also found on

iguana: *The near eradication of the Jamaican iguana (Cyclura collei), now found only on Goat Island (in Old Harbour Bay) and in the Hellshire Hills of Clarendon Parish, is a prime victim of the ecological havoc man has wreaked on the island. Originally hunted by the Arawaks, who prized its succulent flesh and eggs, the introduction of the mongoose by Europeons has further depleted its numbers.*

Hispaniola, is the smallest bird on the island. The extraordinarily plumed Jamaican tody is known as the "robin redbreast." About the size and shape of a wren, it's a brilliant grass-green with a white breast; a patch of bright red feathers surrounds the throat. The rare crested quail dove or mountain witch combines bronze, cinnamon, purple, and black colors with a shaggy grey crest. The plaintive call of the solitaire can be heard high in the mountains. There are two varieties of parrots: the bright green-black and the yellow-billed. The John Crow or turkey buzzard is commonly seen hovering above. The Greater Antillean grackle (locally known as the tinkling grackle) often sneaks scraps from visitors at hotels. The grey Jamaican nightingale is identical to the mockingbird of the American South. Migratory birds include the petchary, bobolinks, indigo bunting, and several varieties of warblers. Introduced birds include the Guiana parrotlet, the saffron finch or wild canary, and the cattle egret from Africa.

reptiles: Jamaican crocodiles (locally known as alligators) live on the S coast. Anole lizards are individually equipped with throat fans of various hues. The croaker, the local version of the gecko, likes to roam up walls while holding on with its suction cup-equipped foot pads. The Jamaican iguana, if not already extinct, is well on its way. The harmless galliwasp lizard, incorrectly identified as poisonous according to local folklore, lives in stony walls and rocky places. The blind worm snake burrows in the ground like an earthworm. A small boa reaches a half m in length. A constrictor which may reach a length of three m (nine ft.), the rarely seen, forest-dwelling yellow snake feeds on rats and birds. The deep-throated toad, imported from the N coast of S. America, is known locally as a bullfrog, though there are no true bullfrogs on Jamaica. There are also a dozen varieties of small frogs which are usually called whistlers or toads. Living high in the trees, the snoring frog is the second largest tree frog in the world.

insects: All told, there are more than 100 species of butterflies or "bats," many unique to the island. The largest of all swallowtail butterflies, the *Papilio homerus* has a wing span of more than 15 cm (six inches). Sought by collectors from all over the world, it dwells in the Cockpit Country and on the most inaccessible slopes of the John Crow Mountains. Jamaica is also home to the world's smallest species of butterfly: its wingspan measures less than a cm. A walking stick known as the pimento horse may reach 22-25 cm (nine-ten in.) in length. The newsbug is a brown scarab beetle which tumbles to the ground when it flies into people, considered a portent of important future events. Fireflies are so huge that they were once captured and worn as living jewels by planters' wives when attending elegant balls held on the sugar plantations. Largest among the 50 species is the click beetle known as the "peenie" or "peenie wallie." Unlike the common fireflies (known as "blinkies"), the peenie has luminous organs located just behind the head. Dragonflies (called "needlecases"), a few scorpions, trapdoor spiders, ants, and termites are also common.

marinelife: The sea around Jamaica is also rich. Many of the more than 50 varieties of coral are unique to the island. Sealife includes the sea urchin, sea fan, blue marlin, and West Indian spiny lobster, and over 800 species of land shells. Green, hawksbill, loggerhead, and the rare trunk turtles inhabit coastal waters, while the pond turtle (actually a terrapin) lives in swamps and ponds. Although manatees are found off the S coast, the West Indian seal is no longer found in Jamaican waters. Its last bastion was the Pedro Cays to the south. Whales and several varieties of porpoises are occasionally sighted off the coast.

sea anemone: *Armed with microscopic stinging cells (nematocysts) on their tentacles, these "flowers of the sea" paralyze small fish and invertebrates and move them back down into their gastrointestinal cavities for digestion.*

HISTORY

European discovery: Human history in Jamaica began when the Arawaks immigrated from the Orinoco region of the Guianas and Venezuela. The first wave arrived around A.D. 650, the second between 850 and 900. At the time of the arrival of Europeans on the island, these coastal, seagoing people numbered 100,000. Although Columbus had heard of the island of *Xaymaca* from Indians on Cuba, he "discovered" the island by accident. Sailing along the S coast of Cuba during his second voyage, he was blown off course and caught sight of Jamaica for the first time. Later that year he set off to explore the island. Arriving on 5 May 1494, he was met by 70 canoes filled with hostile warriors. Columbus and his three caravels paid no attention to them and continued to advance, and most of the Indians fled; Columbus then used his interpreter to reassure the men in one of the canoes. He anchored at St. Ann's Bay, which he named "Santa Gloria" for the beauty of the landscape. Searching for a sheltered harbor in which to repair their ships, they found the mouth of the Rio Bueno. When Columbus ordered a boat

to approach the shore, natives in a canoe came out and attacked it with blowdarts, but were repelled. When the ships anchored at the new location, hordes of curious Indians arrived; Columbus ordered his troops to open fire with crossbows, and an attack dog was set loose. The next morning, however, the Indians returned bearing bammy, fish, and fruit, and begged Columbus not to go away. After finishing his repairs and enjoying some rest and recreation, Columbus and his men sailed on 9 May to the W, where he discovered *Golfo de Buen Tiempo,* the site of present-day Montego Bay. He named the island "St. Jago" or "Santiago" after St. James.

Spanish rule: Returning nine years later, Colombus became stranded at St. Ann's Bay for one year after his two caravels sank. The first Spanish settlers, arriving in 1510, set up the small settlement of *Sevilla la Nueva* near St. Ann's Bay. Its unhealthy climate forced them to move to the place now known as Spanish Town. The Spanish enslaved the native Arawaks and, 100 years later, there were only 74 left. Succeeding them were black slaves from Africa, the first of whom arrived in 1517. The Spanish, eager for slaves to work in the gold mines of Hispaniola, decimated the native population through savage conditions and introduced diseases, to which the Indians lacked immunity. Ironically, the introduction of the first Africans as slaves was prompted by a Catholic priest, Bartolomeo de Las Casas, who was concerned about the potential extinction of the native population. He believed blacks were hardier than the Indians, and that it would be more humane to use them. Too late, de Las Casas realized his mistake. As many as three million people may have been imported from Africa over the following three and a half centuries. Many died in the bowels of the slave ships and countless others from the effects of their harsh living conditions. The Church gave its blessings ostensibly because slavery brought the heathen African under the umbrella of Christian guidance and would increase his chances for salvation. Moreover, the Spanish clergy defined the institution as one ordained by divine law. The British Society for the Propagation of the Gospel even owned slaves in the West Indies. Sugar was the oil of that era, but the Texas oilmen of their time, the plantation owners, were culturally backward to the extreme, and few of the fruits of European culture made their way to the Caribbean. Nothing much happened to the island during the years of Spanish rule, and except for some place names, there are few reminders of their presence. For the Spaniards, Jamaica was basically a base which supplied provisions to Spanish ships and exported lard and hides. Colonists were chiefly farmers and ranchers. A Spanish governor ruled the island in consultation with a *cabildo* (council).

captured slaves being driven to the coast: *One of the little-known ironies of history is that African chiefs didn't hesitate to sell their own people to slave traders. Often, villages would be set afire at night, and the inhabitants would be captured trying to flee. Between 1690 and 1820, 800,000 slaves were imported to Jamaica. Seventeen out of every hundred slaves shipped died within nine weeks of capture. If the "Middle Passage"—the journey by slave ship—didn't do them in, then the "seasoning" did. Not more than half lived to be put to work in the fields.*

British takeover: Pirate ships, covertly supported by European powers envious of Spain's hold on the Caribbean, began arriving during the early 1500s, and overt raids by French and English forces continued into the mid–1600s. On 10 May 1655 a large British expeditionary force sailed into what is now Kingston Harbour and anchored near Caguaya (Passage Fort), which serves as the harbor for Spanish Town. The populace, however, had already fled to the N coast and then on to Cuba. The angry English destroyed much of the town. Slaves, freed and armed by the retreating Spaniards, fled into the mountains and became the Maroons. In 1658 the Spanish attempted to retake the island, and their attack at Rio Nuevo on the N coast on 27 June was the most important battle ever fought in Jamaica. Though the Spaniards were soundly defeated, the war stretched out for two more years before the island was officially ceded to the British Crown in 1660 under the Treaty of Madrid. In August 1660, troops led by colonels Raymond and Tyson mutinied at Guayanoba Vale, 15 km from Spanish Town. (Although reasons for the mutiny are unclear, it's thought to have been directed against the officious D'Olyley and continued military rule.) In 1661 the English appointed D'Olyley the first governor of Jamaica.

buccaneers and slaves: Port Royal emerged as a home base for buccaneers. Before the 1692 earthquake completely destroyed it, Port Royal had become world-renowned as the Sin City of its day. Leader of and most famous of all the buccaneers was Henry Morgan, a Welshman. Shortly after the earthquake, a Spanish fleet invaded the island. This severely damaging attack was repelled at Carlisle Bay, Clarendon. During the 18th

A rare print of the legendary Blackbeard (Edwin Teach), who spread terror throughout the Antilles from 1713 to 1718. The pirate, who wore his long beard tied in pretty ribbons, carried lighted fuses behind his ear so as to always have tinder on hand for his blazing pistols. Pardoned by the corrupt governor of North Carolina, he settled down briefly and married a 16-year-old girl before resuming his murderous calling. When he was finally taken in 1718, his head was cut off and hung as a trophy from the mainmast of his ship for all to see.

C., Jamaica was plagued by pirates, including the legendary Blackbeard (Edwin Teach) and Calico Jack (Jack Rackham). Under the Treaty of Utrecht in 1713, Britain took over France's *Asiento* or contract for providing slaves to the Spanish W. Indies settlements. Soon, slaves were being shipped to the Spanish Caribbean in British-manned boats. In April 1782, British Admiral Rodney intercepted and defeated a combined French and Spanish fleet on its way to attack Jamaica while it was still off the coast. Near the end of the 18th C., Horatio Nelson, later to become

IMPORTANT DATES IN JAMAICAN HISTORY

1494: 5 May. Christopher Colombus anchors at St. Ann's Bay.

1510: Spanish establish settlement of "Sevilla la Nueva" near St. Ann's Bay.

1517: First black slaves from Africa arrive on the island.

1658: 27 June. Battle of Rio Nuevo between the Spanish and the English.

1660: Jamaica ceded to the English under the Treaty of Madrid.

1692: Port Royal destroyed by earthquake.

1760: Coromantee slave Tacky leads slave rebellion near Port Maria.

1831: Slave uprising in Montego Bay led by black preacher "Daddy" Sam Sharpe.

1865: The bloody Morant Bay Rebellion takes place.

1872: Capital moved from Spanish Town to Kingston.

1914: Marcus Garvey organizes the United Negro Improvement Association [UNIA] headquartered in Kingston.

1938: Violence and rioting erupt between workers and police during industrial strikes at Frome, Westmoreland. People's National Party founded by Norman Washington Manley.

1943: Jamaica Labour Party founded by Sir Alexander Bustamante.

1958: 3 Jan. Jamaica enters the West Indies Federation.

1960: 19 Sept. Jamaica withdraws from the West Indies Federation.

1962: 24 April. Jamaica becomes an independent dominion within the British Commonwealth.

1966: 21 April. Haile Selassie arrives on a state visit.

1981: Robert Nesta Marley dies.

one of Britain's greatest military commanders, visited the island. In 1739 and 1740, treaties were concluded with the Maroons which gave them some measure of regional autonomy. The sugar industry came into its own during the late 17th and early 18th centuries. Sixty-six times the size of Barbados (where the sugarcane economy had originated), Jamaica had 430 sugar estates by 1739. Of the tens of thousands of slaves imported to Jamaica during the 18th C., approximately 5,000 remained. In 1760, Tacky, a Coromantee slave, led an unsuccessful slave rebellion in the Port Maria area. Other revolts followed. The final slave uprising was led by "Daddy" Sam Sharpe, a Baptist preacher, in Montego Bay during Christmas of 1831. Although

the composition of its constituency had changed dramatically, the oligarchic system of government remained intact. Its rulers were members of an elite completely out of touch with the rest of society. The Morant Bay Rebellion, led by Paul Bogle, was the culmination of all the discontent. (See "Morant Bay" under "Around The East Coast.") Although the revolt ended in failure, it led to the recall of the governor and the revamping of the constitution to Crown Colony status. The capital was moved from Spanish Town to Kingston in 1872.

the twentienth century: Jamaica was hard hit by the Great Depression of the 1930s. This depression, coupled with the devastation of the banana industry by

Panama Disease, led to the outbreak of violence and rioting at Frome, Westmoreland, in 1938. Out of this chaos emerged the workings of the island's first labor unions and political parties. The Industrial Trade Union was led by Alexander Bustamante, and the socialist People's National Party (PNP) was founded by socialist lawyer Norman Manley. Labor leaders pressed for increased wages, improved working conditions, and political reform. The new Constitution of 1944 allowed for full adult suffrage. The island had become virtually self-governing; only defense and international affairs were taken care of by Britain. The tourist industry, bauxite mining, and industrialization began to flourish.

The long overdue 1954 constitution transferred political power from the hands of the colonial governor into those of elected representatives of the people. The PNP won the next election in Jan. 1955, and in 1958, Jamaica became a founding member of the ill-fated, 10-member West Indies Federation. Continually rent with conflicts almost from its birth, Jamaica was frequently at odds with other members. Contending that Jamaica was under-represented in the Federation which had its capital at Port of Spain, Trinidad, 1,000 miles away, Jamaica pulled out in 1961 after a referendum was held. On 6 August 1962 Jamaica became independent.

zemi: *Carved in shell or stone and found in archaeological digs all over the Caribbean, these idols date from about A.D. 200. Spirits were believed to reside in the idols, which were kept in homes and by Arawak priests. In return for being respected and provided with food and other offerings, the* zemi *was expected to help ensure good hunting, lessen the pain of childbirth, and make crops grow.*

GOVERNMENT

The oldest and strongest democracy in the Caribbean, Jamaica is also the most contentious. No subject in Jamaica is so stormy, so volatile, as politics. Any visitor to Kingston will note the spray-painted slogans which denote the areas divided into "PNP zone" and "JLP zone." Politics is a passion with Jamaicans, and polarization between the two parties makes the Republicans and the Democrats in the U.S. seem like good buddies by comparison.

political structure: After independence in 1962, Jamaica was established as a unified monarchial state. A governor general, recommended by the prime minister, represents the queen as head of state. The bicameral Parliament consists of a nominated Senate and an elected House of Representatives. Although the Senate was originally intended to be a forum of distinguished citizens which could view governmental policy with objectivity and equanimity, this has not happened. Instead, it has become a watering hole where retired politicians are sent before going to heaven or where newcomers can practice before proceeding on to the elected action down below in the lower chamber. Members of the House of Representatives—which holds the real power—are elected by Jamaicans aged 18 or older in each of the 13 parishes and the two corporate areas of Kingston and St. Andrew. The Cabinet, which is the main instrument of policy, is headed by the prime minister. Also the leader of the Opposition, he may appoint 13 of the 21 members of the Senate. The Jamaican legal system, based on English common law and practice,

*Norman
Washington
Manley
(1893-1969)*

is administered by a Supreme Court, a Court of Appeal, and other courts.

political parties: First to evolve was the People's National Party (PNP). Founded by nationalist lawyer Norman Washington Manley, the party had its beginning in the 1938 industrial strikes. Although Manley was involved at the time in representing the industrial estate owners at the trial of the strikers, he threw himself into the task of getting his cousin, Alexander Bustamante, out of jail. He ended up settling the strike masterfully and founded the People's National Party in Sept. of that same year. Bustamante founded the Bustamante Industrial Trade Unions (BITU) in May, and put his full support behind the newly founded party. Feeling alienated from the intellectual leadership, Bustamante drifted away from the party and resigned the next year, claiming it was too radical. From 8 Sept. 1940 to 8 Feb. 1942, Bustamante was again imprisoned by the governor when he threatened to call a general strike. After his release, Bustamante lashed out at the PNP leadership and founded the Jamaican Labour Party (JLP) in 1943 in time for the first election held under the new constitution. In the Dec. 1944 elections, the JLP trounced the PNP. Although the PNP won a plurality of the popular vote in 1949, the JLP won 18 seats to the PNP's fourteen. Bustamante and the JLP swept the 1959 elections but remained the minority party in the federal Parliament because Manley's West Indies Federal Labour Party hit it big in the other islands. Neither Manley nor Bustamante held seats in Parliament, preferring to posture themselves as aloof observers. After continual challenging of Jamaica's membership in the Federation by Bustamante, Manley called for a referendum to decide the issue. On 19 Sept. 1961, the JLP won out and preparations were made for independence.

Sir Alexander Bustamante (1884-1977)

post-independence politics: In the first post-independence elections, held on 10 April 1962, the JLP made a triumphant return to power as it swept 26 of the 45 parliamentary seats. After the 80-year-old Bustamante fell ill in 1964, he was replaced by Donald Sangster who was elected in 1967 only to die in turn soon afterward. (Norman Manley retired and died in 1969, and Bustamente died in 1977.) Sangster was succeeded by trade unionist Hugh Shearer. In 1972 the reins of power passed to the PNP's new leader, charismatic Michael Manley, Norman Washington's son. Promoting himself as a modern-day Joshua, Manley flashed his "rod of correction" (received from Haile Selassie during a visit to Ethiopia) and promised to work miracles. He soon embarked on an ambitious policy of reform. In an attempt to establish what Manley termed an "egalitarian society," state control of the economy was increased, foreign ownership of agriculture and industry reduced, and grass-roots participation in the decision-making process was encouraged. New laws established a minimum wage, severance pay, and maternity leave. Rural areas were electrified, rural health clinics established, thousands of low-cost housing units were constructed, and farm land was redistributed. Manley's policies worked well at first, but they were often conceived and implemented without regard for their wider political and economic consequences. By establishing relations with Cuba, 140 km to the N, and declaring his support for "democratic socialism," Manley managed to alienate both the local elite and foreign investors in one stroke. This spurred the loss of badly needed expertise and foreign exchange with N. America, as well as a drop in U.S. aid. Reminding the middle class that five flights a day left for Miami, Manley encouraged their exodus. The influential Chinese-Jamaican community dropped from 40,000 to 4,000 members by the end of the decade. As conditions continued to worsen, Manley enacted a Ministry of National Security Act, resulting in the formation of the Gun Court which had jurisdiction over all cases involving illegal possession or use of firearms. In order to protect witnesses, press coverage of the juryless trials was forbidden. Until Jan. 1976, a conviction drew a sentence of indefinite detention inside Kingston's Gun Court prison. A National Emergency was declared by Manley in June 1976. Although the island's economy was already in a tailspin, Manley won the 1976 elections handsomely with a four to one victory, and the situation continued

to decline. Led by international reggae superstar Bob Marley, the "One Love" concert, held in April 1978 to commemorate the 12th anniversary of Ethiopian Emperor Haile Selassie's Jamaican visit, helped forge a truce in the bitter political struggle, which lasted two years.

the 1980 elections: But in Oct. 1980, accelerated deterioration in the economic and social situation forced Manley in Jan. to call for elections — two years before his term expired. Fearing violence or a coup d'etat, thousands left the island. Their fears were not unjustified. In June the Jamaica Defence Force, led by Charles Johnson, civilian leader of the small, right-wing Jamaica United Front Party, staged an unsuccessful coup attempt. The election proved to be the bloodiest in the nation's history. Gang warfare raged nightly in the ghettos of Kingston, and the sound of M-16 rifles and Belgian .9 mm stun guns echoed through concrete corridors turned battleground. Landing at a JLP waterfront dance site in rubber rafts, paramilitary troops opened fire. A dozen teenagers were cut down in what became known as the Gold Street Masssacre. By election day at the end of Oct., the death toll had risen to 750. During the course of the campaign, Edward Seaga accused Manley of being a Communist, and Manley countered by accusing the JLP of working with the CIA to destabilize his government. Both politicians survived the bullets fired at them, and with a total voter turnout of 87 percent, 58 percent voted for Seaga and the JLP.

the Seaga era: Born in Boston but raised in Jamaica, Seaga, a Harvard-trained economist who served as finance minister under Bustamante, soon set about putting Jamaica's house politically right. After kicking the Cuban ambassador off the island, he paid a courting call on newly elected American President Ronald Wilson Reagan and was received with great enthusiasm. Seaga's election caused a growth of confidence in Jamaica, but, after an initial upswing, things began to deteriorate again (see "Economy"). In the fall of 1983 Seaga stunned the PNP when, in answer to one of their roll calls for a vote of confidence, he called for snap elections. Riding a popularity wave stemming from Jamaica's high profile in the farcical but popular Grenada invasion, Seaga slated elections for 15 Dec. 1983. This announcement caught Manley unprepared. Claiming that he had received a "solemn pledge" from Seaga that no elections were to be held until the new voter registration list was completed, Manley and the PNP boycotted the elections. As a result, Seaga and the JLP now hold all 60 seats in Parliament. Although the distribution of voter I.D. cards, based on the new lists, has already been completed, Seaga maintains there will be no early elections and "the next general election will be at the latest January 10, 1989." Delivering a major speech in front of the Jamaican Defence Force (JDF) in 1984, he stressed the need for "more discipline in the society." Noting the unique choice of audience for such a pronouncement, the PNP's P.J. Patterson quickly challenged the Prime Minister's remarks. Although the PNP is still registered as a legal political entity, the future of parliamentary democracy in Jamaica is very much up in the air.

coat of arms: *Before Jamaica gained its independence in 1962, the island's coat of arms bore the motto "Both Indies serve One Master." The current slogan is intended to reflect the unity of Jamaica's people despite their racial diversity. Ironically, the Arawaks, pictured on either side of the shield, are no longer with us to share the benefits of this diversity.*

ECONOMY

During the mid-'60s Jamaica was said to have had one of the most promising economies in the Caribbean. Yet, at the same time, it had one of the greatest disparities in income levels of any nation in the world: the upper five percent received 30 percent of the national income while the lowest 20 percent received two percent of the total. Today, that gap still exists, and it has been compounded by a US$2.3 billion debt which Jamaica can barely service, let alone repay. What has happened is that the elite of the society have attempted to live it up like their richer northern neighbors without the financial resources to do so. Jamaica has always been (and is still primarily) a plantation-style economy: exports have served to underwrite imports. In colonial Jamaica, slaves had to cultivate provision grounds, their own small plot of land, in order to help feed themselves. The surplus was sold to women called "higglers" who would resell the goods at the market. Surprisingly, along with 18th C. methods of agricultural cultivation, this system remains intact. To this day, higglers form the backbone of the internal marketing system. Higglers, however, have expanded their role and now board jets bound for Miami, Panama, and Port-au-Prince to buy goods. Returning to the island, they sell these for a substantial profit. Goods are imported in this seemingly ridiculous fashion because the government refuses to issue import licenses for them. Fundamentally a black market economy, Jamaica's most important export, ganja, is illegal (see "Ganja"). The rest of the economic sector can best be divided into bauxite, manufacturing and tourism.

bauxite: One would never imagine that reddish rock could work economic miracles, but this ore plays a major role in the island's economy. Although bauxite had been discovered on the island as far back as 1869, it did not attract attention until the demand for aluminum increased greatly during WW II. Alcan, Reynolds, and Kaiser started production during the 1950s, and by 1957, Jamaica had become the number one bauxite producer in the world, with five million tons of ore or nearly 25 percent of the world's total. By 1975, there were five alumina refineries on the island, and Jamaica had become the world's fourth largest producer and second largest exporter of alumina. It had, however, dropped behind Australia and Guinea in terms of ore production. Jamaicans, on the other hand, were hardly making a heap of money from all of this digging up of the countryside. The original contract specified revenues of only one shilling a ton! When the contract came up for renegotiation in 1957, 11 shillings a ton was agreed upon. Yet, the government collected only US$25 million in 1973 for production of nearly 13 million tons of ore. Jamaica's leaders had discovered that, because bauxite is not labor intensive, it employs relatively few people. Although US$300 million was invested from 1950 to 1970, only about 6,000 permanent jobs had been created. Using a system known as transfer pricing, companies were undervaluing the price of the ore and reducing royalties and tax

Jamaican bauxite workers

payments to a minimum. In order to rectify this situation, a bauxite levy, which indexed the price of bauxite to seven and a half percent of the price of aluminum ingot, was legislated in 1974; it multiplied revenues sixfold. Additionally, 51 percent of Kaiser's and Reynold's local mining operations were nationalized. Following this, the aluminum multinationals reduced production of bauxite and alumina and reduced imports by a third. Meanwhile, curiously enough, strikes increased fourfold. Although the levy was lowered in 1979, Jamaica had started a trend: Brazil and Australia now require that 50 percent of all mineral-based industries be owned by nationals. In 1980, bauxite accounted for nine percent of the gross domestic product (GDP). Today, bauxite production is in decline because a lack of good wars and increased Brazilian production have reduced the price for aluminum. Yet, bauxite reserves on the island are still plentiful. It's estimated that, given current output of 12 million tons per year, supplies will last for the next 150 years.

manufacturing: Although most goods are imported, there is a small manufacturing sector. Since the 1950s, companies— mostly American—have been invited to establish factories, including light industries and assembly plants. However, Jamaica's 80 percent literacy rate, historically strong labor movement, and relatively high wages (compared to its neighbors) have deterred those companies seeking a fast buck. During the 1958-1968 period, the working population increased by 100,000, but only 13,000 were employed by incoming foreign firms. Unable to buy spare parts or raw materials, many factories closed. Most manufactured goods are plagued by high prices and poor quality.

tourism: After Cuba became off-limits for rich American tourists in the 1960s, Jamaica soon became one of the more popular substitutes. Between 1964 and 1974, tourism more than doubled; in 1983, 750,000 tourists visited Jamaica. Unfortunately, because tourism requires large imports of food and other materials, most locals never benefit from the tourist trade. Yet tourism is highly productive in terms of government revenue, and Seaga's current plans call for the establishment of gambling casinos and another doubling of visitors which will involve an investment of over US$575 million.

economy under Michael Manley: All but the most partisan observers concede that Michael Manley's tenure (1972-1980) fell just short of being a total disaster for the economy. While some of the blame may be laid upon the intransigence of the International Monetary Fund (IMF) and skyrocketing oil prices, Manley was clearly at fault by attempting too much too soon and with too little organization to make it work effectively. Self-reliance is certainly a virtue, but it will not happen overnight. And it cannot be achieved, certainly, if industries and utilities are nationalized overnight and the elite driven away like unwanted lepers. His bauxite levy was a brilliant gamble, and without it, the economy would be much worse off today. On the other hand, he spent the revenue on public employment and welfare rather than on building up basic services and industries. By 1980, the GNP had dropped 20 percent, inflation had risen to 27 percent, the level of foreign debt had reached US$1.3 billion, and it was rumored that the economy was propped up only through sales of ganja.

economy under Seaga: Seaga's administration began with an aura of hope. At first Seaga seemed to be successful in turning the country around: inflation declined to five percent, the construction industry revived, and the tourists returned. Money poured in from the IMF and the World Bank. However, things soon took another turn for the worse. And for the poor, life became and continues to be more difficult. Price controls were phased out, rent control ceilings eliminated, and public housing received a low priority. Although Seaga may believe in the "trickle down" theory of economics, the tap seems to be turned off mighty tight at present. While meat, fish, clothing, and canned and frozen goods are at New York City price levels, a new car from Japan is exorbitant. Yet, the minimum wage is still set at an absurdly low J$40

for a 40-hour work week, and a Nov 1982 survey showed that nearly 50 per cent of all Jamaican wage earners received *less* than that. In Jan. 1983 Seaga set up a parallel market for foreign currency which was designed to counter the black market. But by issuing licenses to importers without providing dollars to buy them with, Seaga gave the black market semi-official status. A steep devaluation of the Jamaican dollar (by 90 percent, to J$3.40-US$1) was the result of an IMF impasse in which a standby facility of US$180 million was issued in exchange for the devaluation. The devaluation resulted in a sharp increase in prices. The first month of 1984 saw a rise of 50 percent in the cost of gasoline, kerosene, diesel, cooking gas, bus and air fares, and cargo rates. Electricity rose 40 percent. The island's fuel bill reached US$850 million in 1983, and the debt service ratio is now 26 percent. Bankers, skittish over the situation in Latin America, are currently refusing loans. Jamaica's current account deficit has reached a record high of US$400 million, and the external debt (1982) is US$2.3 billion. Further economic declines have triggered an increase in social tension: several days of rioting spread across the island in mid Jan. 1985, after prices for gasoline and other fuels rose by an average of 21 percent. Coming on top of a 50 percent rise in price for basic commodities during the past year, this proved to be too much to bear. Ten people died in three days of rioting, and banks and businesses in Kingston were closed. Unless a miracle occurs, and a massive change takes place in the world economic order, Jamaica's future appears grim indeed.

AGRICULTURE

Nearly 60 percent of Jamaica's population lives in rural areas, but the island's agricultural economy has always been geared toward export crops rather than production for local use. While the bulk of the sugar, pimento, bananas, citrus, coffee, and cocoa are exported, rice is imported from Guyana, and corn and wheat come from N. America. Of Jamaica's 159,000 farmers, 113,000 work less than five acres each. While the average holding of large farms (500 acres or more) is 2,293 acres, the average peasant must grow what he can on 1.55 acres. A mere half percent of farm operators control 55 percent of the land, including some of the best acreage. Although the rural sector provides jobs for 37 percent of the population, it contributes only eight percent of the GNP—making it the most inefficient sector within the economy. Agricultural methods used by the Jam-

aican peasant have not changed in the past century. Most export crops are in decline. Jamaica had the largest banana export industry in the world until 1937, but production and demand have slacked off in recent years. The sugar industry, single largest employer in the country, is in deep trouble. Since 1974, the world price of sugar has dropped from US$0.65 to US$0.08 per pound, resulting in a massive loss of income. Jamaica produced 192,737 tons of sugarcane in 1983. Although it has an annual export quota of 125,000 of these with W. European markets, inefficient production methods are driving costs up. With US$52 million being spent to modernize sugar mills, British consultants Tate and Lyle have been brought in to streamline management. The continued devaluation of the Jamaican dollar against the British pound has meant a loss of US$22 million

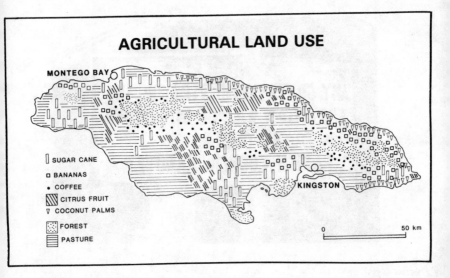

AGRICULTURAL LAND USE

MONTEGO BAY

KINGSTON

▯ SUGAR CANE
▫ BANANAS
• COFFEE
▨ CITRUS FRUIT
▽ COCONUT PALMS
▨ FOREST
▤ PASTURE

0   50 km

in 1982 for agricultural exports to Britain. Under the Manley administration, traditional agriculture grew at a rate of seven percent per year. The Seaga administration seems determined to stress export-oriented agriculture at the expense of local production. In 1983 the government introduced Agro 21, a program designed to raise agricultural imports for N. America, including such unorthodox crops as flowers and exotic spices. Meanwhile, local agriculture suffers. Whereas Manley leased land to small farmers and protected them against imports, Seaga has phased out price supports and allowed unrestricted food imports. Overall domestic food production has plummeted by 19 percent, and the food import bill risen to US$200 million, an absurd amount for a country as fertile as Jamaica. An unrealistic plan by the Seaga administration calls for a reduction of the annual food bill by US$72 million: a harvest of 13,000 tons would be required in 1986, although Jamaica has never produced over 1,650 tons in the past.

GANJA

Ironically, Jamaica's major export crop is one which is legally prohibited. The Indian term *ganja* is used in Jamaica to describe marijuana because that's where it originally came from. After the abolition of slavery in 1838, Jamaica's great sugar plantations needed labor; indentured servants from India began arriving in 1845. Secreting it inside their baggage, they brought the herb with them and shared it with their black co-workers in the field. Its use quickly spread all over the island. It was legal until 1913, when the jittery white ruling class, vastly outnumbered by blacks, enacted a bill outlawing the practice of *obeah* (white magic), informal black militias, and ganja smoking. Informal tolerance, however, continues to this day. The reasons for this are multifold. Although it would be relatively easy to terminate export on such a small island, the government has made only token ef-

forts at eradication. It would not be economically expedient to destroy such a lucrative source of income, which brings in an estimated US$200 million in revenues yearly and provides the sole source of income for tens of thousands. Jamaica shipped an estimated 1,750 tons in 1983, supplying 11-13 percent of the U.S. market's needs. Although the Jamaican Defence Force on occasion blows up some of the estimated 120 or more illegal airstrips (many of which are situated on government land), approval by the government is said to reach right to the top of the bureaucratic hierarchy. It's also believed that doctors, lawyers, diplomatic corp members, and other respected, upper-crust community members are involved in trafficking. They supply the financing, while the estimated 8,000 large-scale growers provide the returns on their investment. The island's largest single cultivator and exporter is the controversial, 2,500-member Ethiopian Zion Coptic Church, a distorted offshoot of Rastafarianism, which has been indicted stateside on charges of conspiracy to import and traffic at least 15 tons of marijuana. Already the island's largest private landowner, its profits have been invested in everything from gas stations to ricefields to coconut cookie factories. According to reports, some police are tolerant because they both use ganja and are on the take. Many police remain silent in return for a cut in cash or herb, and in some areas, they are reportedly the largest dealers. It's also a common practice for police to confiscate ganja with the intention of reselling it themselves. In December 1983, three plainclothed policemen were brutally murdered when they attempted to confiscate a ganja crop in Westmoreland Parish. Locals contended that they had no idea that the interlopers attempting to take away the product of their sweat were officers of the law.

cultivation: In some communities more than 25 percent of the households openly cultivate ganja. Cultivation for export is time-consuming, expensive, and risky. Plants must first be sprouted in a nursery before being transferred to the fields where they are continually watered, weeded, and fed with organic fertilizers. Besides taking care to avoid the prying eyes of the police, cultivators must also guard against birds and insects. Because growers rarely dare to take the time or have the necessary knowledge to cure their crop properly, the quality of even the best Jamaican marijuana compares unfavorably with top-grade Mexican, Hawaiian, and American varieties.

use: Ganja is in common use in Jamaica; more than 60 percent of the lower class ingest the herb in one form or another. It may be used in tea, steeped in white rum or wine, cooked in food, or smoked. Even upper-class Jamaicans, who disdain ganja smoking as a lower-class habit, regularly ingest it as a tea or tonic; it's maintained that these strengthen the blood, enabling it to stave off disease. It is also used to induce sleep, and in rural areas as a salve for infected wounds and allergic reactions. Considered an herbal medicine rather than a drug, Jamaican men smoke ganja rolled into five-inch paper or cornhusk *spliffs*. Contrary to the popular misconception that ganja induces a state of indolent, slothful somnolence, it actually produces an energy burst sufficient for completing arduous tasks such as field work with greater speed, enabling them to work longer and harder than they would otherwise. Ganja provides a buffer against the agonizing monotony of field labor. Not only do some Rastafarians smoke an incredible amount of ganja, but it's considered vital to their religious practices; they claim it is the herb specified in the Bible. Perhaps this idea of sanctity, like ganja itself, comes from India where it's also used in Hindu rituals. In any case, Rastas swear by their weed.

finding it: Ganja is far from being difficult to obtain in Jamaica; in fact, it would be difficult to walk around anywhere in the tourist belt or even in the countryside and not be approached by someone wishing to sell it. Prices range from J$1 for a small quantity to J$20 for 50 grams or so. As with anything else, the higher the quality the higher the price. Every village or town has a ganja bar, yard, or camp where the herb, both loosely packaged and rolled into *spliffs,* is sold alongside bottles of beer and stout. *Sinsemilla (sinse* for short) is a Spanish term used to denote the highest quality weed, which is further divided into different qualities such as Lamb's Bread, Burr, and the exceedingly rare Coton. Other grades include Goat's Horn, Mc-

Coney, and Collie or Kali; Bush and Mad are the lowest potency grades.

warning: One should be cautious about using ganja because legal penalties are stiff. Under the Revised Dangerous Drug Act, a first-offense conviction for possession can bring up to a J$2000 fine which may be coupled with a jail term of up to seven years. Second offenders may be fined J$5000 and imprisoned with hard labor for up to 10 years. Dealers or cultivators may receive five to 10 years in prison with hard labor. Needless to say, Jamaican jails are hardly fun places. Despite the economic importance of the drug, it is unlikely that there will be any lessening of penalties or legalization in the near future. Without the U.S. paving the way first, the Jamaican government would be unwilling to undertake such a controversial move. Additionally, damaging side-effects might occur: ganja prices might go into a tailspin, severely disrupting Jamaica's black market economy which is dependent upon regulated funds from ganja imports for financing purchases from abroad.

THE PEOPLE

FOREIGN INFLUENCES

Caribbean culture is truly creole culture. The word "creole" comes from *criar* (Spanish for "to bring up or rear"). In the New World, this term came to refer to children born in this hemisphere, implying that they were not quite authentic or pure. Later, creole came to connote "mixed blood," but not just blood has been mixed here: cultures have been jumbled as well. Because of this extreme mixture, the Central Caribbean can truly be called a cultural goldmine. The culture of a specific island or nation depends upon its racial mix and historical acculturation. Beliefs were merged in a new synthesis—born of the interaction between different cultures—African and European. Today, many traces of influence remain in terms of language, society, crafts, and religion.

native Indian influence: Although the Indians have long since vanished, their spirit lives on—in tradition, in the feeling of dramatic sunsets, and in the wafting of the cool breeze. Remaining cultural legacies include foods and dishes (such as "bammy" on Jamaica); many place names and words (such as "hammock"—an Indian invention); and in native medicines still in use. Many Spanish towns were built on old Indian sites; the *bateyes* of the Indians became the plazas of the Spanish. There are numerous archaeological sites, most notably those at Utuado and Tibes in Puerto Rico.

African influence: Probably the strongest of all outside influences. The arriving slaves had been torn away from both tribe and culture, and this is reflected in everything from the primitive agricultural system to the African influence on religious sects and cults, mirroring the dynamic diversity of W. African culture.

Spanish influence: The original intruder in the area. Although the Spaniards were routed from Jamaica relatively early, it still retains its Spanish legacy in the form of such obscure things as place names and in "escovitched," the Spanish way of marinating fish. Most Caribbean islands, whether Spaniards ever settled there or not, still bear the names Columbus gave them. Major Spanish architectural sites remain in the old parts of San Juan, Puerto Rico, and Santo Domingo, the Dominican Republic.

British influence: Still dominates the governments, societies, educational systems, language, and judicial institutions in Jamaica and the British Virgin Islands, and other former and present colonies.

French influence: Although Haiti has been independent more than 150 years, French mores and values still dominate Haitian institutions to a surprising extent. Although less than 10 percent of all Haitians speak French fluently, French is the official language of Haiti. Most of the social and artistic mores of the upper classes are as well, and many a Haitian leader has seemed to be a caricature of Napoleon. To the S, Martinique and

Guadeloupe are still departments of France.

American influence: Something you'll find when and where you might least expect it. American presence in Puerto Rico and the Virgin Is. predates American ownership of these islands; television and fast foods have served to increase it. Jamaican reggae musicians (like the original Wailers) started out crassly copying American R&B. American interventions in the Dominican Republic and Haiti left influences which persist to this day; much of the Haitian road system was built by American engineers. And, when hundreds of thousands of Haitians take to the seas, risking death and deportation, they too are pursuing the American dream of "life, liberty, and the pursuit of happiness."

Blue Mountain girl carrying mangoes

THE JAMAICANS

Although one gets the impression from Jamaica's motto ("Out of many, one people") that the country's society is composed of a number of groups living together harmoniously, such is not the case in reality. Of 2.1 million Jamaicans, 97 percent are black. Although 18 percent of these are considered to be "coloured," only three percent are o Eurasian stock and of these, only one percent are white. Thus, Jamaica is a predominantly black island with a population composed largely of the descendants of slaves, and this continues to mold the social structure. Of the Eurasian minority, influential far beyond their numbers are Indians, Chinese, and Lebanese (called "Syrians"). Beneath them on the social hierarchy are the mulatto ruling class which was created under British rule and survives intact to this day. In this stratified society, being white is often seen as being rich. (The only poor whites on the island are a group of German descent who reside in Seaford Town.) While the rich pursue their dream of "the video and the Volvo," the poor are left to just barely scuffle by. For the upwardly mobile, it is an asset to be able to document some trace of European ancestry. Jamaicans may destroy snapshots of themselves if they appear too dark in them, and newspapers have been known to flatter or malign public figures by lightening or darkening photos. This type of cultural schizophrenia is a direct result of the legacy of colonialism and reflects the fact that a secure Jamaican identity has not yet emerged. Among Jamaican blacks, skin color and physiognomy vary. This is because Jamaicans come from a variety of different tribes—Ibos, Yoruba,

Mandingoes, Bakongo, Ashantis, Fantis, and Fulas—to name a few.

population: A million or more Jamaicans live in the U.S., mostly in the New York City or Miami areas; a similar number are in Britain, Canada, and other Commonwealth countries. Although the average populaton density for the entire island is about 477 persons per sq mile, most habitable portions of the island have 1,000 or more persons per sq mile. More than 37 percent of all Jamaicans now dwell in urban areas, and the slums of Montego Bay and Kingston are crammed with over *25,000* people per sq mile.

male and female relationships: Jamaica's matriarchal society has its roots planted in tradition. In some African societies, matrilineal by custom or otherwise, the sexes are independent of one another. African women and their children spend their lives separate from their husbands and fathers. Wives have their own hut or room, and may own property individually. The effects of 179 years of slavery added to these customs has helped bring the present system of Jamaican social relationships into effect. During British rule between occupation and abolition (1655-1834), male slaves were allowed relationships with females only for the purposes of procreation. Prohibited from establishing long-term relationships, a male might be sold away and never even cast eyes on the child he'd fathered. As a consequence, children were largely raised by their mothers. This system of casual alignments continues to this day. The grandmother plays a vital role in the family. The custom of the grandmother helping out came about during the days of slavery, when a mother might be sold without her children; the grandmother would then take over their care. Today, a grandmother may look after her daughter's children or even those of her son. If a daughter does not wish to be burdened with the children from a previous relationship, she may ask her mother to take care of them. After a time, she may come to retrieve them. Sometimes the mother goes out to work so that the grandmother may remain at home with the children. This type of family pattern exists not only in Jamaica, but wherever slavery has been in existence in the New World.

families: The average Jamaican lower-class family usually lives together for a long time before they get married if, in fact, they get married at all. Contributing to this is the high cost of a wedding ceremony and reception coupled with a lack of tradition of formal marriage ceremonies. As a consequence, 40-70 percent of all births occur out of wedlock. Sex is considered to be a natural function which should not be repressed; male potency and female fertility are viewed as status symbols. A woman in her 20s who has not had a child is referred to as a "mule" (mules are sterile). Thus, over one-third of the live births in Jamaica occur among unwed teenage mothers, and the island population continues to explode. Having a child may be a way to insure a steady income, and in many cases, a woman's sole income may come from child support. In the so-called "keeper family," a man and a woman will live together. Thrown largely on his own resources, the Jamaican male has had to use a combination of his own wits and trickery to survive. The woman may go out to work, and the man may not assert authority as the woman may break away at any time. Under the "twin household" plan, a man may set up a second household with another woman at the location where he is working.

LANGUAGE

JAMAICA TALK

origins: But Jamaicans speak English don't they? Yes, but it's not quite as simple as all that. Populated by African slaves from many tribes who had to learn to speak English in order to communicate among themselves and with their overseers, Jamaica has developed its own uniquely colorful dialect. Unlike St. Lucia, where there are strong French influences in the native Creole, or Trinidad which has Spanish as well as French influences, Jamaican English has been influenced predominantly by W. African languages, notably Twi and Ashanti.

grammatical structure and language content: Both have been affected and shaped by the whims of historical circumstance. As no formal schooling was allowed under the slave system, Africans learned English in the field directly from their overseers, thus creating a unique blend of African and British grammatical structures, language content and intonation. "D," for example, is substituted for "th" as in "dat" for "that," and "de" for "the." Some aspects of intonation seem to be connected with Welsh as well, as in the dropping of the "w" sound in "woman" (pronounced "ooman") or the pronunciation of little as "likkle." Because of the immense distance from Britain, many words from Elizabethan English remain: jugs are still called goblets, small bottles are vials, and married women are referred to as Mistress instead of Missus. African influence is clear in the grammatical practice of reduplica-

tion, evident in regional dialects. A *bo-bo* is a foolish person, *bata-bata* means to beat repeatedly, and *njaka-njaka* means untidy or slovenly. More than 400 words of African origin are in use. *Duppy,* the word for ghost, derives from the Twi word *dupon,* which means the roots of a large tree. *Nyam* means "to eat," while *duckonoo* is the Gold Coast name for a dish of boiled corn. The Jamaican imagination has added many new colorful words and expressions to the English language. "Soon come" means eventually something will arrive or occur, while "walk good" is a farewell greeting. *Bangarang* is baggage; *fish-head* is a bribe, and *horse dead* and *cow fat* are irrelevant details. Jamaican speech is the product of a society stratified by more than 400 years of colonialism. Although slowly changing, the only socially acceptable speech among the Jamaican upper classes is BBC English. Middle-class Jamaicans will speak Creole only to their inferiors, consciously or unconsciously slipping back into standard English while addressing social equals.

Rasta influence: Jamaican language has been further enriched and enhanced by the introduction of Rastafarian dialect into general usage. "Irie" is now commonly used upon departing, while curse words popularized by Rastafarians, such as *bomba clot* and *rhas clot* (meaning "ass cloth"), and *pussy clot* and *blood clot* (both connoting the local equivalent of menstrual pads) are all too popular, as the rantings of any irate male will demonstrate. In Rasta talk, first person singular is always expressed as "me" and pluralized by "I-n-I." The addition of "I" in front of words (see chart) serves to increase identification with self and with Haile Selassie ("Selassie I"). If you should be asked, "Where the I live?", it means "Where do you live?"

CAPSULE RASTA TALK

Armageddon: the final battle between good and evil as predicted in the Bible.

Babylon: used to mean either the established order (Church and State), or the police or a policeman.
bandulu: criminal or bandit; hustler.
bredrin: brethren of the Rastafari cult.
bull bucka: a bully.

chalice, clutchie: the Indian chillum, a ganja pipe.

dedders: meat.
Downpressor: oppressor.
dread: may mean dreadlocks, courage and fearlessness in the face of obstacles, or a dangerous or serious situation.
dreadlocks: the distinctive Rasta locks; a person wearing these locks.
dreadnut: coconut.
dunza, dunzai: money.

Elizabitch: Queen Elizabeth of England.

firstlight: tomorrow.
firstnight: last night.
fire, fiyah: Rasta greeting.
fullness: state of being full, absolute, complete.

ganja: marijuana.
gates: Rasta home.
groundation: large Rasta gathering.

hail: Rasta greeting (from "Haile!" of Haile Selassie).
hard: proficient, skilled, excellent.
herb: marijuana.

I 'n' I: I; we.
irate: create.

irey, irie, iry: Rasta greeting; state of being in tune with nature, in harmony with the universe.
isire, izire: desire.
I-tal: natural foods, cooking, purity, natural style of life.
itches: matches.
ites: Rasta greeting meaning "may the receiver attain spiritual heights."
iwer: power.

Jah: Jehovah, God.
Jah-Mek-Ya, Jamdung: Jamaica.

kingman: male spouse (the king of a wife is her husband).

lion: righteous male Rasta.
lovepreciate: appreciate.

natty, natty dread: dreadlocks.
negus: king.

one love: parting expression meaning unity.

pollution: the masses of humanity living in spiritual darkness.

Rahab: the U.S.
roots: Rasta greeting; native, natural, derived from communal experience.

satta: invitation to sit; meditate, rest.
screw: to be angry.

upfull: upright.

wolf: Rasta imposter.

yood: food.

Zion: mythical Africa; Ethiopia.

RELIGION

For most Jamaicans, religion is much more than just paying lip service to vague ideals; it represents a total involvement, a way of life. One may literally eat, drink, sleep, and dream religion. As is true in poor Third World countries throughout the world, religion is very important because only religion provides respite from the constant difficulties and struggles of everyday life. For people living in acute poverty, anything which gives comfort or a hope of rising from the surrounding squalor is welcome. Major religious sects in Jamaica include the Baptist, Methodist, and Anglican churches. The United Church of Jamaica and Grand Cayman is the result of a 1965 union between the Congregational Union and the United Church of Jamaica. Others denominations include Moravians, Quakers, Roman Catholics, and a small number of Jews. Although Christianity forms the religious model for society, many African elements have crept in.

Christianity: As with culture in general, religion throughout the Caribbean is a combined affair, with an icing of Christianity laid on top of an underbelly of animistic rituals and beliefs imported from W. Africa. The planters—concerned more with material than spiritual benefits—saw little incentive to introduce the slaves to the wonders of the Christian God. On the other hand, depending only on fear to keep the masses of slaves in line, the masters viewed the emergence of cults with a cautious eye. Slaves could be driven to revolt by leaders who promised them immunity from bullets. Such a threat to authority had to be kept in line, and cults were rigidly suppressed. Christianity became a convenient cover for African religion, and indeed, was considered compatible by the slaves. The cults have had a longer run than the slave masters and still command considerable influence everywhere save the Virgin Islands. Although cults like Rastafarianism bear little resemblance to

African religious practices, they have deep underlying African roots.

CULTS

Bedwardism: Because established religion has tended to butter its bread on the side of the government and formal religious practice was actively discouraged by the slave owners, cults have always been an important outlet for religious expression. One of the earliest of these was Bedwardism, which centered around the messianic folk hero Alexander Bedward (1859-1930). Born in Jamaica, Bedward emigrated in the 1880s to Panama where he had a religious vision which prompted him to return to Jamaica. In 1886 he was baptized by H.E.S. Woods, popularly known as "Shakespeare," and entered the Jamaica Native Baptist Church in August Town, St. Andrew. Beginning his own ministry in 1891, his fame spread far and wide. As his popularity as a healer and preacher grew, so did scrutiny and concern on the part of British authorities. Arrested for sedition in 1895 after he prophesied that blacks would crush whites, he was committed to a lunatic asylum. Released after his lawyers intervened, he remained active until his prediction that he would ascend to heaven on 31 Dec. 1920. Selling their homes and belongings, thousands of followers from Jamaica, Cuba, and Central America flocked to August Town. Needless to say, the expected miracle failed to occur. On 21 April 1921, he led his followers on a march to Kingston where he was re-arrested and again committed to the asylum, where he died in 1930.

black and white magic: Although Bedwardism is defunct, many other colorful cults are still in existence. *Myal, obeah,* Convince, and *Kumina* all have African roots; *myal* and *obeah,* black and white magic respectively, are the most direct manifestations of African religion in Jamaica. Now virtually extinct as distinct cults, various elements from them have been adopted by the Afro-Christian sects. The name *myal* comes from the word *maye,* meaning sorceror or wizard. The most important function of myalism was healing through the use of herbs and holding ceremonies at the base of *ceiba* (silk cotton) trees where *obeah* and *myal duppies* reside. While *obeah* men and women would be called upon to place spells, *myalists* would be called in order to hold ceremonies to counteract them. *Obeah* (from the Akan word *abayi,* meaning "sorceror") still enjoys a measure of underground popularity. Science, a new form of *obeah,* is based upon the magical and mystical tracts (banned in Jamaica) published by the De Laurence Company of Chicago, Illinois.

Bongo: An *obeah*-related cult is the Convince cult. Nicknamed "Bongo" and strongest in St. Thomas and Portland, it originated among the Blue Mountain Maroons. Men and spirits are seen to be co-existing within a single, unified social structure. Interacting with one another, they influence each other's behavior. Spiritual power is seen as morally neutral, and ghosts are called upon to help the living. Some are from Africa; others derive from the ancient Jamaican slaves and Maroons. At ceremonies, ghosts take possession of their devotees. Spirits enter devotees in order to further their own selfish ends; lacking a body, they long to speak, smoke, dance, and sing. Each has its own personality and idiosyncrasies. Upon possession, the face of a devotee contorts into a grimace. Ghosts may curse unrestrainedly, finger themselves through their trousers, make lewd propositions, even chase women through the yard and attempt to rape female devotees. Being possessed by a spirit has its drawbacks: hot-tempered spirits treat their borrowed bodies roughly, and may even cause physical injury or death.

***Kumina* or *Cumina*:** Another cult that stems directly from *obeah*. Begun by Free African migrants from the Congo, its name derives from the Ki-Kongo word *kumina* (to move with rhythm). Built upon a ritual dance which accompanies exorcism, this ancestor worship cult believes that proper ceremonies must be held for the dead in order to ensure that their *duppies* will not wander about wreaking havoc. Ceremonies are held on special occasions such as rites of passage, or times of illness in the community. Services are accompanied by dancing and drumming. The larger *kimbandu* and the smaller *kyas* are the two types of drums played exclusively by males. Dancing to the drums continues until a devotee is possessed by spirits and delivers a revelation from an ancestor. The revelation may be uttered in local dialect, or in a language incomprehensible to all but those persons in trance. A goat may be sacrificed during the ceremony.

revival movements: Jamaican Revivalism started at the beginning of the 19th C. when W. African religious beliefs were merged with those of the Baptist faith to form new sects. These began to flourish during the Great Revival of 1860-61 when many Revival groups were started by established ministers. (Alexander Bedward was also shaped by this movement.) As is the case with the other sects described above, Revival sects are spirit

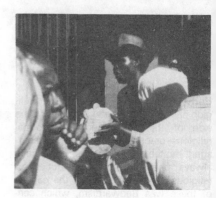

streetside revival meeting in Spanish Town

cults; their members are possessed by guardian spirits who perform consultations and oblige favors in return for food. The two major sects are Pocomania and Revival Zion. Both share many common characteristics. Both sects have leaders (called "Shepherd" in Poco and "Captain" in Zion; female leaders are called "Mother"). Both sects hold meetings of their "bands" in a "mission ground" or "seal ground." Leaders wear turbans and are known for their ability to prognosticate. The main difference between the two sects lies in the type of spirits they worship. While Zion deals only with "heavenly" spirits (God, angels, saints, and archangels), Poco deals with "ground spirits" (the dead) or "earthbound spirits" (fallen angels). In general, Revival Zion, led by the flamboyant dean of Jamaican art, Kapo (Mallica Reynolds), is much less African influenced than the often disdained Pocomaniacs. Although rituals may vary between the two sects, "trumping and travailing" in the spirit is a common denominator. Deities are African gods that have been renamed Michael, Satan, Gabriel, Jesus Christ, etc. Although many of the cults described above are gradually dying out or losing ground to Rastafarianism, anyone who doubts their influence should take a stroll in or around any of Jamaica's major produce markets where cultists are frequently in evidence.

RASTAFARIANISM

Most famous (and at times in the past, infamous) of all the sects originating in the Caribbean, Rastafarianism is also the most horrendously misunderstood. Although it has an estimated membership of just over 100,000, imposters are rife. Dreadlocks alone do not a Rastafarian make. Although their appearance may be forbidding, Rastafarians are gentle, spiritual people who really do believe in "peace and love." The name itself stems from *Ras,* the title given to Amharic royalty, combined with *Tafari,* the family name of the late Ethiopian emperor Haile Selassie; the term Rastafarian thus denotes a follower of Ras Tafari or Haile Selaisse.

origins: Marcus Garvey introduced the ideas that were to become embodied in Rastafarianism. Garvey sought to unite blacks under the cry of "One God! One Aim! One Destiny!" His ultimate ambition was to return to Africa, the fatherland. In 1914 he organized the Universal Negro Improvement Association (UNIA). Headquartered in Kingston, its professed goals included a worldwide unity of the black race, the economic and social development of Africa into a model in which all black people could take pride, the development of black colleges and universities, etc. Finding he had little effect upon the middle-class Jamaicans, Garvey emigrated to the U.S. in 1916. His newspaper, *Negro World,* spread his views, capsuled as "Africa for Africans at

Home and Abroad" and "Up, you mighty race, you can accomplish what you will," to 40 countries. His ideas made enemies in the European colonial and American establishment who had mineral and commodity-producing interests in the countries where he was most popular. Both integrationist blacks and communist sympathizers criticized him for not following their ideologies. In 1922 he was set up by the American government on a mail fraud charge and served two and a half years in prison in Atlanta before having his sentence commuted and being deported back to Jamaica in 1927. Garvey moved his UNIA headquarters from Jamaica to London in 1935. He died there in 1940 without ever having visited Africa. In a church in Kingston in 1927, Garvey prophesied that a black king would be crowned in Africa. In 1930 Ras Tafari, the great grandson of King Saheka Selassie, was crowned emperor of

Marcus Garvey

Ethiopia. Taking the name Haile Selaisse ("Might of the Trinity"), he further embellished his title with epithets like King of Kings, Lord of Lords, His Imperial Majesty the Conquering Lion of the Tribe of Judah, and the Elect of God. The Ethiopian Christian Church, of which he was a devout member, considered their kings to be directly descended from King Solomon. In the midst of a severe economic depression, Jamaica in 1930 was ready for a new religion. Promoted by early leaders such as Leonard Howell, Rastafarianism soon gained currency among the rural and urban poor.

cosmology: Comparatively speaking, Rastafarianism may best be likened to a black version of messianic Judaism, or fanatical Christian sects still found in the U.S. today. The parallels are striking. Haile Selassie is the Black Messiah, and Ethiopia is the Promised Land. God is black, and Rastas are one of the lost tribes of Israel. They have been delivered into exile through the hands of the whites and are lost wandering in Babylon, this "hopeless hell," known to the world as Jamaica. The ultimate goal is repatriation to Ethiopia where they will live forever in heaven on Earth. The goal of repatriation, however, has now been modified. As this is realized to be an impossible goal under prevailing circumstances, the current belief is that the status quo on Jamaica must be changed first. Ras Samuel Brown, the 1960 candidate of the Black Man's Party, was the first Rasta candidate to compete within the electoral system. Though defeated, his challenge earmarked a change in attitude.

Selassie's Jamaican visit and death:
When Selassie arrived at Norman Manley International Airport on 21 April 1966, he was greeted by thousands of Rastas who

were smoking ganja and chanting "Jah Rastafari!" Selassie immediately retreated into his plane and shut the door. Neither Selassie's lack of support for Rastafarianism, nor the military coup which deposed the Ethiopian king in 1975, failed to dampen the spirits of ardent believers. The military leaders accused Selassie of letting 100,000 peasants die during the course of the most severe drought in Ethiopia's history. (Despite Rasta theology, Haile Selassie was one of the worst tyrants in African history.) After the deposed emperor died in a small apartment inside his former palace in Addis Ababa on 27 Aug. 1975, Rastas either refused to face the facts, or portrayed Selassie as a living god who had simply moved on to another plane of existence. This follows a pattern typical of messianic cults throughout the world in which the leader lives on in the spirit after his death.

membership composition: Members are young, with over 80 percent in the 18-35 age group. Although Caucasians in general are considered to be the personification of evil, whites are considered and judged on an individual basis; many American whites have joined the sect and have been fully accepted. Women are relegated to a minor role; their only functions are housekeeping, selling crafts, etc. During the past 20 years, Rastafarianism has permeated the middle class as well as every ethnic group, but believers are still predominantly composed of the urban have-nots. Rastas are prominent among dissenters from established societal groups. The religion offers a spiritual and ideological alternative which sets its members apart from the system itself.

rituals, taboos, and symbolism: Rastas are basically vegetarians. Vegetables, fruit and juices are dietary staples. Fish less than a foot long may be consumed, but shellfish, fish without scales, and snails are prohibited. Rastas prefer to eat *I-tal* (natural) foods, and they avoid cooking with salt and oil. They strongly object to cutting hair or shaving. Although Rastas are nonsmokers and teetotallers, their consumption of ganja is legendary. Its many names ("wisdom weed," "wisdom food," "the healing of the nations") express the reverence that Rastas feel for this plant. The very act of smoking is considered to be a religious ritual. Like the Catholic communion cup, the pipe Rastas use to smoke ganja is known as a chalice. Rastas usually pray to Jah Rastafari or recite variations on verses taken from Psalms 19 and 121 before smoking "the herb." They also cite other biblical passages which they believe sanction and sanctify the smoking of ganja. (Not all Rastas smoke ganja however, nor is it necessary to smoke ganja in order to be a Rasta.) Rastas claim they suffer no ill effects even after decades of continued daily usage. Indeed, they maintain that they are healthy *because* they use ganja. Although not all Rastas wear locks and not all wearers are Rastas, dreadlocks are seen as connecting the Rasta with the Ethiopian lion; Rastas cite biblical passages (Leviticus 19, v. 27; Leviticus 21) to support this practice. The lion is a symbol of Rastafarianism, and as a representation of Haile Selassie, the Conquering Lion of Judah, it may be seen everywhere. Rastas represent the spirit of the lion in the way they carry themselves, in their locks, and in their challenging attitudes towards contemporary social values. Their colors—red, black, and green—are the colors of the Garvey movement: red represents the blood of Jamaican martyrs, black is the color of African skin, and green represents the vegetation of Jamaica as well as the hope of achieving victory over the forces of oppression. *Nyabingi* is a Rastafarian convention, a gathering of the tribe to mellow out together, which may last anywhere from one day to a week. April 21, the date of Haile Selassie's visit, has become a high holy day for the movement.

attitudes toward Christianity: Christianity is regarded with the greatest suspicion. Even though some Rastas have become members of the recently introduced Ethiopian Orthodox Church, many have already quit out of disillusionment. The white God of the Christians is regarded as a dangerous deceiver because his religion denies blacks their rightful destiny (to rule the earth) and expects them to be humble while awaiting death and the passage to an imaginary heaven. For the Rasta, heaven is attainable here and now.

relating to Rastas: Their disturbing dreadlocks and their consumption of marijuana have often served to invoke fear. Several incidents in which Rastas shot police and soldiers have also reinforced this false image. Despite this, Rastas are congenial, gentle, and trustworthy people. The *true* Rasta, that is. Beware of "wolves in sheep's clothing," Jamaicans who seek to exploit the popularity of Rastas and reggae by adopting Rasta fashion without Rasta content. As a general rule of thumb, the closer you are to tourist traps like Ocho Rios and

Negril, the greater the ratio of fakes and hustlers to genuine Bible-thumping Rastas. Real Rastas prefer to stay out in the country and avoid contact with the pollution of Babylon. If you want to establish whether a Rasta is for real or not, note what he says, what he eats, or what he smokes. If he tries to hustle you for bread, eats meat, or smokes cigarettes, chances are good that he's not the genuine article. In general, check out the quality of the Rastaman vibration you're receiving.

Blue Mountains Rasta: Many Rastas shun the hustle and bustle of city life, preferring a meditative existence in the country.

MUSIC

The roots of Jamaican music are sunk deeply in the history of Caribbean colonialism. The ethos of musical expression in Jamaica—indeed, in black music in the Americas as a whole—stems from the struggle of a people wrenched out of their own cultural milieu and thrown into unfamiliar circumstances as well as with strangers of diverse cultural backgrounds. The only possession the Africans could bring with them was the space inside their heads; slave owners had no control over cultural memories. But even these memories, already dulled by the cruel voyage overseas and the horror of slavery, were further confused by the mingling of members from various tribes. As is so often the case in the Caribbean, a cultural synthesis emerged which forged the old into the new. What the slaves could remember, they practiced—often in the face of prohibition (playing drums, for example). What could not be remembered or only half remembered they improvised and expanded, often merging African and European elements. The music of Jamaica is an expression of the adaptation to a foreign, inhospitable environment. What is so remarkable about Jamaican music, in light of this, is its joy and vigor—in the captivating melodies of mento and calypso, in the vibrant and assertive spirit of reggae. Like American gospel, it expresses spiritual triumph in the face of hardship. Unlike gospel, blues, and jazz, which share the same roots, Jamaican music frequently includes biting social criticism and sarcastic commentary which has often been subject to the censure of authority.

history: It's impossible to evaluate contemporary Jamaican music without considering its past. Work songs were among the earliest musical developments. Part singing and call-and-response chanting were of African origin, consisting of verses led by a *bomma* with the *bobbin* (responding chorus) answering at the end of each verse. (Currently, these are kept alive only in the performances of respected Jamaican musicologist Olive Lewin and in the music of the singers of the National Theater Dance Company.) Jamaica's organized musical history begins with the slave orchestras, formed by some of the wealthier planters, which would perform on slave holidays such as Picaninny Christmas, and End of Crop Time. Another form, the quadrille, was the Jamaican equivalent of the Spanish *Bomba y Plena* and the kissing cousin of the American square dance. Bands consisted of fiddle or violin supplemented with trumpet or fife. Introduced by the planters, slaves took the quadrille to heart and soon made it their own. Deeply influenced over the years by its American counterpart, Jamaican music flourished, producing mento, then ska and rock steady, before proliferating internationally with the development of reggae.

calypso and mento: Contrary to popularly held opinion, calypso is not indigenous to Jamaica but is an invention of Trinidad. This fallacy was fostered because calypso, having gained popularity abroad, was promoted by Jamaicans to encourage tourism. Songs like ''Jamaica Farewell'' and ''The Banana

and W. Indian slums of London until Millie Small's Chris Blackwell-produced hit "My Boy Lollypop" made it an international sound for a brief interim. Ska was supplanted around 1966 by rock steady, the forerunner of reggae.

REGGAE

'One good thing about music, when it hits you feel okay"
—from *Trenchtown Rock* by Bob Marley

You don't try to understand reggae; you feel it. It's not head music; it's music which hits you in the gut like a shot of raw rum. More than anything else it's a distillation of the Jamaican ethos: the sounds of the city and country, the vibrations of an island that is at once mellow and intense. Both music and lyrics reflect the realities of modern life in Jamaica. And, as such, they reflect the aspirations and struggles of Third World people everywhere.

Boat Song" ("Day-O"), popularized by Harry Belafonte, were actually written by Irving Burgie, a Brooklyn native who studied at Juilliard. Mento, on the other hand, *is* a Jamaican original. While some mento songs dealt with sad or nostalgic occasions, others were adaptations of old British folk songs or sea shanteys. Often plaintive and slow, its lyrics leaned toward the ribald rather than the political. Unlike the succinct and politically pungent content of calypso, mento dealt primarily with Caribbean sexuality in a forthright manner. Church censorship forced record sales under the counter. Instrumentation was simple: guitar, bongos and shakers, with a rhumba box—a large, wooden box straddled by the musician who plucks the four metal strips which substitute for strings. Regrettably, its 2/4 rhythm, once the mainstay of every dance or social event, has all but died out.

ska: A creation of the sound studios which invented the dance craze of the same name, ska was the early '60s Jamaican music—disorganized but cheerful and funky. Its popularity remained limited to the ghettos of Kingston

roots: No one is quite sure exactly from where reggae music appeared. If anything, the development of reggae is linked inseparably to the maturation of the Rastafarian movement. Rasta drumming comes from Kumina drumming which, in turn, comes from Africa. The late Count Ossie and his band, the Mystical Revelation of Rastafari, were the precursors of reggae. Their songs incorporated *burra* and *funde* drumming with the sustained two-beat riff that supplies much the same trancelike effect as reggae. Reggae may be defined as the synthesis of electrified African music coupled with the influence of ska, rock steady, and American rhythm and blues.

CONTEMPORARY
REGGAE
STARS

Bunny Wailer

Rita Marley

Eek-a-Mouse

Mutabaruka

Judy Mowatt

Yellowman

Toots Hibbert of Toots and the Maytals claims to have originated the term in his song "Do the Reggay." Certainly the Maytals were and still are one of the most important reggae groups, but their producer Clement Dodd also claims responsibility for the development of the music. Producers like Lee Perry and Island Records owner Chris Blackwell, however, have certainly had an important hand in molding the music: both helped shape the most influential band of them all, the Wailers.

the Wailers: Some give the Wailers credit for transforming reggae into its present format. Originally formed in the mid-'60s as the Wailing Rude Bwoys, the band contained Bob Marley, Junior Brathwaite, Peter Tosh, and Bunny Livingston. As they began to gain popularity in 1972, three other members were added. Despite the presence of two tightly produced, classic albums on the American market, the band became popular largely from British rock superstar Eric Clapton's cover of Bob Marley's "I Shot the Sheriff." (Needless to say, not many overseas listeners picked up on the fact that the song, dictated in Jamaican patois, was the story of a confrontation between a ganja farmer and the police.) The major label distribution and promotion of *Catch A Fire,* coupled with the American release of the Jamaican film (and accompanying soundtrack), *The Harder They Come,* had a steamrolling effect on the band's popularity. No sooner had the Wailers grown popular than its members went their separate ways, with Marley changing the name to Bob Marley and the Wailers. By the time of his death from brain cancer at the age of 36 in 1981, Robert Nesta Marley had become an international superstar. His influence on the music remains strong to this day. More than anyone else, he made reggae synonymous with Rastafarianism and social protest.

technique: The steady thump-thump-thump of the electric bass complements the chika-chika-chika staccato scratch of the guitar and the choppy drum sound. The resulting sound—unmistakable and instantly recognizable—resembles riding seas of rhythm with vocals supplying the melodies. Solos are not factored in, and jams are multi-instrumental funk sessions. A development that is affecting other types of music as well is the dub. Dubs originated as the flip side of singles in which the vocals had been mixed out and replaced by enhanced bass and drums along with echo techniques. The deejay and the dub poet, who talk, sing, and rap over the background music, are a direct result of the development and continued popularity of dubs.

current performing artists: Reggae has become thoroughly internationalized, and there are now reggae bands everywhere from Japan to Europe. In fact, some of the major sounds in reggae today come from Britain: Steel Pulse, the most highly acclaimed contemporary reggae band, hails from there, as does the formidable dub poet, Linton Kwesi Johnson. While some musicians have emigrated, others, like Jimmy Cliff, have returned to the island after long stays abroad. Hottest rhythm section on the island is bassist Robbie Shakespeare and drummer Sly Dunbar. Dubbed the "Riddim Twins," Sly and Robbie formed an integral element in the major reggae band Black Uhuru. Roots Radics, having backed many Jamaican artists, is the Muscle Shoals rhythm section of reggae, playing on numerous studio records. One of the most popular reggae singers is Dennis Brown who is backed by Lloyd Parks and We the People; Gregory Issacs, the "Cool Ruler," has been responsible for many hits. Dub poet Mutabaruka remains the performer considered most likely to take up the Marley torch. Inside Jamaica, however, he has been upstaged by the flamboyant Yellowman (Winston Foster) whose deejay rap songs deal with themes dear to the hearts of most Jamaicans: sinsemilla and sex. Hot island bands include Third World, Chalice, Culture, the Mighty Diamonds, and Toots and the Maytals. Many Marley associates and offshoots continue to produce fine music. Among these are ex-Wailers Peter Tosh and Bunny (Livingston) Wailer; the former I-Threes, Bob Marley's backup vocalists continue to make albums and solo appearances as Rita Marley, Judy Mowatt, and Marcia Griffiths.

the future of the music: In the '80s reggae has begun to have more and more of a mass audience appeal. Many white rock bands like the Police, UB40, and Blondie, which have incorporated reggae into their music, enjoy a wider popularity than any native reggae band has had or is ever likely to enjoy. Ironically, much of the music is losing its social content as artists discover that they prefer Volvos to vehemence. Steel Pulse has toned down its lyrics in an attempt to secure a wider audience appeal; other acts have followed suit. Since the demise of Bob Marley and the defeat of Prime Minister Michael Manley and the PNP in the 1980 elections, the music, although continuing to mature and grow, is losing its rebel stance. While Bob Marley has been promoted to demigod status (and has become as commercialized as laundry detergent in the process), no island successor has emerged to claim the vacant throne. In fact, the major voice of social protest is British dub poet Linton Kwesi Johnson, who, ironically, has disavowed both the rigors of Rastafarian rigamarole and the title of reggae artist. (He considers himself mainly a poet.) Other acts, like the comical Eek-A-Mouse, are of value more for their entertainment than for their lyrical and musical backbones. Despite this, Jamaica still seems to have deep reserves of talent. One thing is certain: reggae will continue to change, diversify, and grow as long as there are people who like to dance.

ART AND DANCE

For such a small island, Jamaica certainly is a wellspring of artistic talent. As any visitor to Kingston's National Gallery will attest, Jamaica has a large number of gifted artists who rival, if not surpass, those of any other Caribbean island, including Haiti. Moreover, it's not necessary to enter a gallery to see art. Art is everywhere, from the wall murals of Tivoli Gardens in W. Kingston to the colorful cartoons which adorn the sides of small restaurants and the carts of vendors all over the island.

artists in Jamaica: Because it was created by and for the British expatriates at the top of the heap, most early Jamaican art reflected the needs and values of the colonial power structure. Examples of this range from the pretentious marble statue of Rodney in Spanish Town—clothing him in a toga as if to claim consanguinity with the Roman Empire—to the formal oil portraits of the plantation owners. With the introduction of nationalism in this century, island art has undergone a dramatic transformation. Most visually dynamic of Jamaica's art styles, the intuitive or "primitive" art resembles that of Haiti. Jamaican works, however, are less stylized and homogenous. The movement began with such artists as John Dunkley and Henry Daley. Dunkley returned in the 1930s from his quest for fortune in C. America, and gained fame after he used his newly opened barber shop as a canvas—covering it with flowers and other patterns before taking off to put his own very special dark and prepossessing pictures on canvas. As the decades passed, the intuitive style of painting has broadened to include Rastafarianism, pastoral, and urban themes. They were followed by ar-

Spanish Town
street art

*"**Miss Lou**": After nearly a half century in show business, Louise Bennett is an island institution. Known as the "Queen of Folklore," Bennett came to fame satirizing everything from political legend Sir Alexander Bustamante to Anancy the Spider to the foibles of the white elite—all within the context of the patois-contrived rhymes written for her pantomimes.*

tists like Evarld and Sam Brown, Allan Zion Johnson, Albert Artwell, Gaston Tabois, and Sidney McLaren. One of the leaders behind this movement has been Edna Manley, a brilliant sculptress, and the wife of Norman and mother of Michael. Other artists of note include Gloria Escoffery, Carl Abrahams, Ralph Campbell, David Pottinger, Albert Huie, and Karl Parboosingh. Far and away the most famous of them all, however, is sculptor and painter Mallica Reynolds, who paints under the pseudonym "Kapo." Leader of the Pocomania sect, he is already something of a folk hero in his lifetime. (See the remarkable special exhibition hall devoted to his work in Kingston's National Gallery.)

dance and drama: The most famous dance and drama troupe is the all-volunteer National Theater Dance Company (NTDC). Unique in the Caribbean, like saltfish and ackee they're a Jamaican specialty. Try to see one of their enjoyable performances which are held from mid-July to Mid-Aug. and in Nov. and December. (A sampler of NTDC's religious works is held at Kingston's Little Theater every Easter Sun. at dawn.) Every dance form is incorporated into their material, set to background music ranging from *Kumina* drumming to Bob Marley. The National Pantomime, now in its fourth decade, opens its season on Boxing Day (25 Dec.) each year at Kingston's Ward Theater. Its topical vignettes artfully satirize current island events. Story lines often spoof Jamaican history while taking a poke at public figures. Even if you can't unravel the patois, it's worth going to feast your eyes on the colorful sets and costumes.

FESTIVALS AND EVENTS

Sadly, many of Jamaica's traditional festivals are on the wane. Hussay or Hosay, an E. Indian festival which used to be a common sight in many towns, can now be found in only a few. And, although "Bruckins Party" is part of the dance competition in "Festival" (see below), this colorful set dance is seldom found on the once prominent holiday of Emancipation Day (1 Aug.).

Festival: Chief event on the island, Festival has broadened beyond its original intention (to celebrate Jamaica's Independence) to include a vast spectrum of events: fine arts, culinary competitions, photography, crafts, fishing regattas. From coconut-husking contests to the hoity-toity Miss Jamaica pageant, everything is included. Although Independence Day is on 5 Aug., it is traditionally celebrated on the first Mon. of the month. A parade held on that day features historical and mythical characters including Anancy, Paul Bogle and George Gordon, and Maroons and Arawaks.

Jonkanoo **(John Canoe):** Although no one is sure what this dancing procession is exactly about, or where and how it originated, the name comes from the Ewe tongue, meaning "deadly sorcerer" or "sorcerer man." Probably it originated in the secret societies of E. Africa and became linked to Christmas, the only major holiday permitted to slaves. Although Jonkanoo is recognized today as part of the island's cultural heritage, such was not always the case. In 1841 riots erupted

Jonkanoo celebrants in Port Antonio

PUBLIC HOLIDAYS

New Year's Day
Ash Wednesday
Good Friday
Easter Monday
Labour Day, May 23
Independence Day (1st Monday in August)
National Heroes Day (3rd Monday in October)
Christmas Day
Boxing Day (December 26)

EVENTS

6 January: Accompong Maroon Festival, Accompong, St. Elizabeth

February: Hague Agricultural Show, Hague Show Grounds, Trelawny

April: World Youth Festival of Arts, Kingston
Jamaica Folk Singers Season, Little Theater, Kingston

11 May: Bob Marley Day, island-wide concerts

July: JCDC Independence Festival, island-wide concerts

5 August: Independence Day Street Parades and Celebrations, Kingston and all Parish capitals

August: Denbigh Agricultural Show, Denbigh Show Grounds, May Pen, Clarence
Reggae Sunsplash, Jarrett Park, Montego Bay
National Theater Dance Company (NDTC) Season, Little Theater, Kingston
The National Pushcart Derby, Kaiser Sports Club, Discovery Bay

September: Annual Port Antonio International Marlin Tournament

October: Jamaica Heritage Week, island-wide celebrations including exhibits and ceremonies

December: Reggae Superjam, National Stadium, Kingston
The LTM Pantomime, Ward Theater, Kingston
Jonkanoo Dancers, island-wide

after Kingston's mayor banned the parade. In succeeding decades it was repressed, until just a few decades ago, when it was again deemed acceptable. But with legitimization has come a corresponding decline in interest, and today, Jonkanoo dancers are no longer a common sight around Christmastime. Bands usually include a cast of colorful characters dressed in flashy rags. Featured may be a cow or horse's head, a king and veiled queen, a devil, and a few Indians. This strangely enchanting amalgam of motley characters wends its way down the road to the polyrhythmic accompaniment of drums and cane flutes.

FOOD

No problem with eating here! Restaurants range from tourist traps and plastic fast-food joints to local dives. The latter are undoubtedly among the best places to eat. Usually the menu is written on a chalkboard inside and changes according to what is available that day. Don't let their appearance (which may be less than inviting) scare you off. Hygienic conditions are reasonably high, so there's no need to worry about getting sick. In small towns, be sure to eat early because restaurants may close early. Strict vegetarians will find a ready refuge in Rastafarian-run *l-tal* restaurants. For N. Americans or Europeans raised on a diet of fast food, Jamaica's cuisine provides a delightful change. And most dishes have a fascinating history behind them to boot, combining culinary traditions of the native Arawaks, W. Africans, British and Spanish to create new types of dishes which are uniquely Jamaican. The piquancy of Jamaica's cuisine dates from the period during the country's early isolation when food shipped in had to be dried, pickled, or salted. Spices were added to disguise that fact or to improve the flavor. Today, these same spices — including pimento (allspice), ginger, nutmeg, and several local varieties of pepper — give dishes their distinctiveness.

APPETIZERS AND SNACKS

appetizers: One of the most unusual appetizers is Solomon Grundy, which is well-seasoned, pickled herring. Another is peppered shrimps. These are small crayfish caught in the streams and rivers of St. Elizabeth and Westmoreland. Boiled with salt and seasoned with local pepper, they are sold at roadside stands. Use Pickapeppa Sauce or Jamaican Hell Fire to spice up your food. Mango Chutney is one of the few remnants of Indian cuisine in Jamaica.

snacks: Roadside stands, which sell a variety of treats depending upon locality, abound along Jamaica's country roads and beaches. Patties, pastries filled with meat and vegetables, are an island staple. Stamp and Go, a name excerpted from nautical commands given to sailors in the days of yore, are fried and crispy codfish fritters. Fried fish and bammy is an adaptation of a native Arawak specialty found on the S coast. Bammy is a fried, pancake-shaped spongy bread. Once the staple food of the poor before flour became readily available, it survives today in a modified, more compact form.

Bulla is a sweet, small, but tough round cake made with flour, soda, and molasses. Fried yams, plantains, and boiled and roast corn are other common snacks. A great way to cool off and gain quick energy is to munch on a stalk of sugar cane artfully peeled for you by an island vendor. Unlike other islands, where pepperpot refers to a cassareep (cassava) stew, pepperpot here is a soup which combines greens, okra, dasheen leaves, and corned beef or pork. Jamaicans also make a great conch soup.

ackee

ackee: Most peculiarly Jamaican of all island foods, ackee and saltfish is usually eaten as a snack or as a breakfast dish. Ackee is boiled together with saltfish or salt pork and seasonings and served with dumplings (fried balls of dough) or as a sandwich. Although ackee is actually a fruit, it is always boiled before cooking in order to release the toxin (hypoglycin) inside. Because of this poison, ackee can only be picked after the pods open

naturally. The pulp or aril must be thoroughly cleaned of red fiber, and cooking water must be discarded. (Ackee is rarely eaten on other islands because others are terrified of the poison.) There are two varieties of ackee: "butter" and "cheese."

desserts: Jamaica's colorfully named desserts and sweets include coconut drops, grater cake, pone pudding, Bustamante backbone, guava cheese, and matrimony. The latter is made with pulped orange and star apples mixed with cream. A feature of Jamaica's innumerable pastry shops is rock bun cookies, which are huge, chewy, and excellent. Mannish water, a tonic served at weddings or on other festive occasions, is a thick, highly seasoned soup which combines green bananas, goat offal, and any available vegetables. Duckunoo or "blue drawers" is an African sweet made of corn flour mixed with sugar and nutmeg, wrapped in a banana leaf, and steamed. The steaming imparts its characteristic dark blue coloring.

MAIN DISHES

Rice and peas is the standard-bearer of Jamaican cuisine. Because of its widespread popularity, it is sometimes referred to as the "Jamaican Coat of Arms." Red or gungo (Congo) peas are mixed with rice, coconut milk, and spices to form this staple dish. Curried goat, introduced by indentured servants from India, is usually served with rice and green bananas. Jerk chicken and pork is made by smoking the flesh over a pimento wood fire; Maroons, who used the method of preparation to cook wild boar, originated this legendary island specialty. The best is found on the E coast at Boston Beach near Port Antonio. Escovitched fish is a Spanish technique in which any large fish is cut into slices and sauteed in a peppery vinegar and onion sauce. Coconut milk is boiled to a custard and mackerel, shad, or cod is added along with onions and scallions to form rundown or run-dun.

DRINKS

Perhaps nothing is more important to the Jamaican than his drink. One of the most notable characteristics of the island is the plethora of shops, bars, and other places serving beverages. Jamaica makes the most famous rum in the world. (In Germany, the name "Jamaica" has become synonymos with rum itself.) Distilled directly from cane in oak barrels, Jamaica's rum runs from light to dark varieties. Jamaicans, however, most commonly imbibe white rum. White overproof is the local, strong white rum. There are also a number of liqueurs, the most famous of which is Tia Maria. The most famous brand is Appleton. Jamaica's local beer is Red Stripe. The same brewers produce Dragon Stout, which competes with locally brewed versions of Guinness and McPherson. There's also a locally brewed version of Heineken (at least what the brewers *claim* to be Heineken). Beer is often drunk at room temperature or "hot." Although Jamaica is famous for its highly expensive Blue Mountain Coffee, Jamaicans, disappointingly, prefer instant. Caffeine addicts might consider bringing their own along with an electric coil. Tea, as the word is used in Jamaica, refers to any hot drink. Teas include dandelion, mint, ginger, fish, ganja, and mushroom. Be wary of the strong effects of the latter two! Fish tea is made from boiled fish broth with green bananas, other season-

CONTENTS: 10 fl. ozs. 284 ml.
Brewed & Bottled by
DESNOES & GEDDES LTD., KINGSTON, JAMAICA, W.I.

ing, and vegetables. Rum punch is made by combining lime juice, fruit syrup, rum, and water. ("One of sour, two of sweet, three of strong, and four of weak" runs the age-old recipe.) Wash is made with brown sugar, water, and lime or sour oranges. The prize for the healthiest drink goes to Irish Moss. Made by combining processed seaweed (agar) with condensed milk, nutmeg, and vanilla, it is believed to aid sexual prowess. A seasonal drink found around Christmas, sorrel is a cheerful, bright red drink made by stewing and sweetening the petals of flowers from the Sudanese shrub.

FRUIT

In addition to commonly known fruits like mango, avacado, paw paw (papaya), pineapple, apple, bananas, guavas, and oranges, Jamaica also has a number of fruits unique to the island. Ortanique, a cross between an orange and a tangerine, was created by Charles Jackson of Manchester Parish; its name is a combination of the words "orange," "tangerine," and "unique." The crimson, pear-shaped otaheite apple was introduced along with breadfruit by Captain Bligh. Underneath its thin skin lies a sweet white flesh which surrounds the seed. Soursop is a sour, prickly fruit used to make a milky soup which has alleged aphrodisiac properties attached to it. Naseberry or sapodilla is a peach-sized brown fruit with an edible skin and delicately flavored pulp. Slightly sweet, nearly seedless, and loose skinned, the appropriately named ugli is a hybrid of a grapefruit and a tangerine. What is called cashew fruit is actually the fleshy stalk below the nut, which is eaten raw, stewed, or boiled. The native star apple is a sweet purple fruit which reveals a star-shaped pattern when cut crossways. The sour pulp of the Indian tamarind tree, extracted by sucking, is a delicious treat. A

hybrid between the sweet orange and the citrus plant "shaddock" from Polynesia, Jamaican grapefruit originated in the W. Indies. Really more a vegetable than a fruit, the starchy, rough and rotund breadfruit is eaten roasted, boiled, or fried. After Jamaican planters, deprived of food during the turbulent years surrounding the American Revolution, heard about the breadfruit tree, they persuaded the king of England to launch an expedition, led by Captain Bligh, to obtain it. His first attempt, on the ship *Bounty*, ended in mutiny. Although he finally succeeded in bringing the tree to the island in 1793, it was many years before it became the island staple it is today.

ugli: A cross between a tangerine and a grapefruit, the loose skin of this hybrid citrus fruit peels to reveal the jucy segments inside.

PRACTICALITIES

GETTING THERE

by air: Jamaica is readily accessible from most cities in N. America. Although the only really cheap way to get to Jamaica is to swim, you can save money by sensibly shopping around. A good travel agent will call around for you to find the lowest fare; if he or she doesn't, find another agent, or try doing it yourself. If there are no representative offices in your area, check the phone book—most airlines have toll-free numbers. In these days of deregulation, fares change quicker than you can say "Jah Rastafari," so it's best to check the prices well before departure—and then again before you go to buy the ticket. The more flexible you can be about when you wish to depart and return, the easier it will be to find a bargain. Some fares are APEX (advance purchase excursion fares)—meaning you must reserve 7-21 days beforehand. Others are open, "no strings, no frills" flights, but are "capacity-controlled," meaning, buy your ticket fast! Whether dealing with a travel agent or with the airlines themselves, make sure that you let them know clearly what it is you want. Don't assume that because you live in Los Angeles, it's cheapest to fly Air Jamaica directly from there. It may be cheaper to find an ultra-saver flight to gateway cities like New York or Miami and then change planes. Fares tend to be cheaper Mon. through Thursday. Although high season is generally from around mid-Dec. to mid-April, fares also increase 1 July to 31 Aug. (around Independence Day) when expatriates return to visit loved ones. The cheapest rate you can possibly hope to get is in the range of US$210 RT (from Canada, about C$359 RT). Air Jamaica flies direct from New York (three hours, 45 min.); Miami (one and a half hours); Toronto (four hours); Los Angeles (five hours); Atlanta (two hours, 45 min.); Philadelphia (four hours); and Baltimore (three hours, 10 min.). Eastern Airlines flies from Miami, Atlanta, and Chicago. They offer a bewildering variety of APEX fares, so do some checking to find the most convenient. American Airlines flies direct only from New York City. Jamaica may also be reached directly from anywhere in the Caribbean except Cuba and the Dominican Republic.

by sea: With the exception of cruise ships, there's no longer any passenger service between Jamaica and other Caribbean islands. And, unless you're willing to take a cruise—which not only costs more than flying but often prevents contact with locals—no other regular transport from the continental U.S. is available. One potentially rewarding opportunity—for those who can afford it—is to sail your own yacht to Caribbean waters and travel about on your own. It's possible to crew on a boat coming over from Europe; most, however, head for the southern Caribbean so you'd have to find a way (rather expensive) up from there.

GETTING AROUND

While not exactly the easiest island in the world to get around on, Jamaica has a reasonably efficient basic transportation network. Minibuses and shared taxis (same charge for both) run along nearly every road on the island, and have nearly

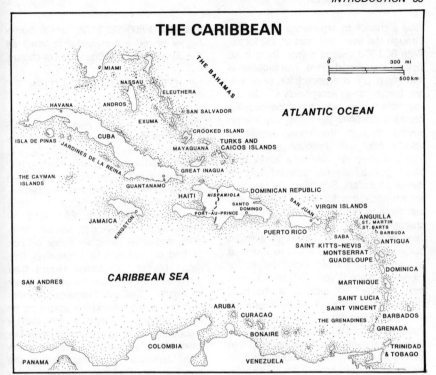

THE CARIBBEAN

ATLANTIC OCEAN

CARIBBEAN SEA

replaced the slow and ramshackle but colorful country buses which are ideal for short hops. Be sure to agree on fares before boarding the minibuses. All taxis sport PPV (public passenger vehicle) plates, except for "contract carriages" which have JUTA painted on them. While JUTAs have fixed fares posted, taxis are metered. Remember that night rates for taxis are higher. Drivers should be tipped. Hitchhiking is quite possible but can be slow owing to lack of traffic. If you're going anywhere off the beaten track, be prepared for a long wait. If you're with a group, it might be wise to combine funds and rent a car for the day. Although gas is expensive (US$2.19 per gallon), you can cover much more area and visit otherwise inaccessible places.

The sole remaining railway service in the Caribbean runs twice daily from Kingston to Montego Bay and back. For specific travel information, see "getting there" for each area.

ACCOMMODATIONS

Range from the very expensive to the very cheap, depending directly upon what standards you wish to maintain. The more flexible you are, the easier it will be for you to find a cheap or relatively inexpensive place. Off-season rates (1 May to mid-Dec.) are usually cheaper, but smaller places may charge the same all year long. By avoiding large hotels, not only will you save money, but you'll also have a chance to experience the country through the eyes and ears of the locals. With 800,000 visitors a year, there is no lack of accommodations. The problem is that most are overpriced for what you get. Larger hotels accept only US dollars, and when you add the bloodsucking hotel tax (US$4-12 per night), you end up paying through the nose. Jamaicans usually stay with relatives when they travel; if they do stay at a hotel, they often get a special reduced rate in Jamaican dollars. Still, there are plenty of accommodations for under US$10; you just have to dig for them. These places charge neither for service (usually 10 percent) or for the hotel tax. Locals will also put you up, but on an island as touristed as Jamaica, it's rarely done except for monetary gain. If you wish to stay in a small village, ask around at the local shops as to whether there are any rooms available. Remember that prices may fluctuate according to currency rates, inflation, and season. Bargaining can often save you money. One solution for travelers with limited time or for those who wish to be sure of finding a place is to hook up with Peter Bentley's Jamaica Camping and Hiking Association (JACHA). Peter has compiled a list of more than a hundred cheap places to camp or stay island-wide. For US$15, Peter will send a booklet, map, and other information detailing camping and budget accommodations on the island (write JACHA, Negril, Jamaica; or c/o Box 216, Kingston 7; tel. 809-927-0357). Peter, a tour guide for SOBEK, also offers three-day Blue Mountain and other hiking tours as well as whitewater canoeing. Although you're likely to pay more if you go through JACHA, it's the cheapest alternative other than fending for yourself. To make reservations from the U.S., phone the Jamaica Reservation Ser-

vice (tel. 1-800-526-2422), which books higher priced accommodation listed by the Jamaica Tourist Board free of charge.

OTHER PRACTICALITIES

shopping: Retail shops are open Mon. through Sat.; in some areas shops close after noon on Wed. or Thursday. Aside from Rastafarian carved, agricultural, and woven products, there isn't much to buy in Jamaica. In fact, as most products are smuggled in from the States to avoid import restrictions, it's better to bring everything you need. Film and all photographic accessories, camping supplies, and other items are either difficult to find or prohibitively expensive. Correctly or not, Jamaicans regard their manufactured products as being inferior in quality. Certainly Jamaica's Comet matches don't even strike sparks so be sure and bring your own. It might also be a good idea to bring in practical items like used clothing, batteries, etc., to trade with. Jamaican rum, acclaimed as the finest in the Caribbean, makes a nice souvenir.

money and measurements: The monetary unit is the Jamaican dollar, which is divided into 100 cents. Bills are 1, 2, 5, 10, and 20 dollars. Although the US dollars. Banks are located in Kingston, higher rate given at the bank makes it infinitely preferable to convert to Jamaican dollars. Banks are located in Kings-ton, Montego Bay, and tourist centers throughout the island. Black market rates run about 10-15 percent above bank rates. The best place to change money is in the tourist shops of Montego Bay. Travelers cheques bring a lower rate than cash. Don't change more than you need, however, because an exchange certificate is required to change money back when leaving the country. Export or import of Jamaican currency is prohibited. Banking hours are 0900-1400, Mon. to Thurs.; 0900-1200 and 1430-1700, Fridays. Although the imperial and

metric systems are in use, the country is gradually being converted to the metric system alone. Road distances are listed in kilometers. Electricity is 110-220 volts AC 50Hz.

METRIC CONVERSIONS

Since this book is used by people from all around the world, the metric system (with feet and miles in parentheses) is employed throughout. Here are the equivalents:

1 inch	= 2.54 centimeters (cm)
1 foot	= .3048 meters (m)
1 mile	= 1.6093 kilometers (km)
1 km	= .6214 miles
1 nautical mile	= 1.852 km
1 fathom	= 1.8288 m
1 chain	= 20.1168 m
1 furlong	= 201.168 m
1 acre	= .4047 hectares (ha)
1 sq km	= 100 ha
1 sq mile	= 2.59 sq km
1 ounce	= 28.35 grams
1 pound	= .4536 kilograms (kg)
1 short ton	= .90718 metric ton
1 short ton	= 2000 pounds
1 long ton	= 1.016 metric tons
1 long ton	= 2240 pounds
1 metric ton	= 1000 kg
1 quart	= .94635 liters
1 U.S. gallon	= 3.7854 liters
1 Imperial gallon	= 4.5459 liters

Fahrenheit / Centigrade thermometer scale:

230° / 110°
220°
210° / 100° Water Boils
200°
190° / 90°
180° / 80°
170°
160° / 70°
150° / 60°
140°
130° / 50°
120°
110° / 40°
100°
90° / 30°
80°
70° / 20°
60°
50° / 10°
40°
30° / 0° Water Freezes
20°
10° / -10°
0°
-10° / -20°
-20° / -30°
-30°
-40° / -40°

to compute centigrade: Subtract 32 from Fahrenheit and divide by 1.8. To go the other way, multiply Centigrade by 1.8 and add 32.
time: To avoid confusion, all clock times appear according to the 24-hour airline timetable system, i.e., 0100 is 1:00 a.m., 1300 is 1:00 p.m., 2330 is 11:30 p.m., etc. From noon to midnight, merely add 12 to regular time to derive airline time.

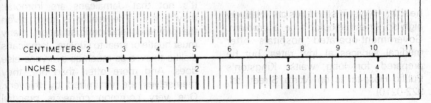

CENTIMETERS 2 3 4 5 6 7 8 9 10 11
INCHES 1 2 3 4

The Sunday Gleaner

1834-1984/150 YEARS

broadcasting and media: Jamaican radio and television are more or less a wasteland, offering little in the way of investigative journalism or innovative, creative programming. Viewed as reactionary by programmers, reggae is seldom heard on the radio; Jamaican radio is most notable for the call-in talk shows which graphically illustrate the where, what, why, and how of daily life and thought processes on the island. Although Jamaica has a free press, it's monopolized by the Gleaner Company—the Rupert Murdochs of Jamaica. Founded in 1834, the *Daily Gleaner* represents the conservative business interests; as it relies heavily upon advertising, it tows the government (Labour Party) line. *The Star* is a tabloid which is the equivalent of the *New York Daily News* in terms of intellectual content.

visas: Nationals of the British Commonwealth, the Republic of Ireland, and the United States may stay up to six months without a visa. Europeans may stay up to three months without a visa. With the exception of Mexico and Turkey, all others require visas. Upon arrival you must have a valid passport, an onward or return ticket, and sufficient funds (this amount may be determined by the immigration officer) for your stay.

health: Hygienic standards are relatively high so illness shouldn't be a problem. Government-operated hospitals offer medical services at low rates, but be prepared for long waits. Kingston's Public Hospital is on North Street (tel. 922-0210).

services and information: Pay phones can be scarce and hard to find. Put in J$0.10 only *after* your party answers. If the coin gets stuck, bang on the phone. Although phone numbers are grouped in three and four digits separated by a dash, the first two digits are the area code. Dial "0" before the number for long distance. For international calls, dial "113" to get an international operator (there's a 50 percent tax on these). Jamintel (Jamaica International Telecommunications Ltd.) has branches in Montego Bay and Kingston; night letters (22–word minimum) or telegrams are half price. Letters are cheap (J$0.20), but it may take a week for one to get from Montego Bay to Kingston. Bring your own envelopes because they cost more than the postage stamps. Have mail sent c/o General Delivery, General Post Office, Montego Bay or Kingston. Small but good parish libraries are found in main towns throughout the island. Deposit J$20 for a temporary membership that enables you to borrow up to three books. Tourist information centers are located in Montego Bay, Ocho Rios, Port Antonio, and Kingston. Ask about their "Meet the People" service which will put you in contact with locals.

theft: Petty thievery is a longstanding Jamaican tradition. Expect this and prepare for it by exercising caution. If you are a white (therefore assumedly rich) visitor on an island which is 98 percent black, you'll stick out like a sore thumb. It's not that Jamaicans are immoral; they're not. The reality is that, given the prevailing economic situation, many must hustle or steal to survive. Jamaicans dislike thieves as much as everyone else does. And more often than not, they themselves are victimized by thievery. One very common crime is praedial

JAMAICA TOURIST BOARD OFFICES

JAMAICA

JAMAICA TOURIST BOARD
EXECUTIVE OFFICE
Government Conference Center
Block 11, 14-20 Port Royal Street
Kingston (809) 922-0131

Cornwall Beach
Montego Bay
(809) 952-4425

Ocean Village Shopping Center
Ocho Rios
(809) 974-2570

City Center Plaza
Port Antonio
(809) 993-3051

Plaza de Negril
Negril
(809) 957-4243

ENGLAND

Jamaica House
50 St. James's Street
London SW1A 1JT, United Kingdom

WEST GERMANY

Goetheplatz 5,6000
Frankfurt/Main 1
Frankfurt

UNITED STATES

866 Second Avenue
10th Floor
New York, N.Y. 10017
(212) 688-7650

36 S. Wabash Avenue
Suite 1210
Chicago, Ill. 60603
(312) 346-1546

1320 S. Dixie Highway
Suite 1100
Coral Gables, Fla. 33146
(305) 665-0557

3440 Wilshire Boulevard
Suite 1207
Los Angeles, Calif. 90010
(213) 384-1123

CANADA

2221 Yonge Street
Suite 507
Toronto, Ontario M4S 2B4
(416) 482-7850

110 Sherbrooke St.
Mezzanine Level
West Montreal, Quebec H3A 169

larceny, or in plain English, crop stealing. Jamaicans have been known to surround thieves and stone them to death. Remember, whatever you have and they don't, they want and may steal to get. Don't flash your money or possessions around. Never leave anything unattended — whether on the beach or inside someone's house. If anything should be stolen, report it to the police immediately.

However, don't expect the venerable redstripes to recover anything. They're more adept at taking bribes from ganja smugglers than at catching thieves. There's very little armed robbery compared to pilfering, so it's always better to carry valuables with you as opposed to leaving them in an insecure place. If camping, don't leave anything inside your tent that you'd mind losing.

CONDUCT

While traveling in Jamaica or any other Caribbean locality, keep in mind the history of the region, and the effects — deleterious or otherwise — of nearly 500 years of colonialism. Remember the injustices wreaked here and don't serve to perpetuate them. Expect to be hustled, especially on the N coast. Don't let them get to you, and don't get angry lest you provide them with some amusement. Generally, Jamaicans are warm, gracious, and friendly people. Cultural differences are occasionally manifested in the language so be prepared and don't misunderstand. For example, calling somebody "white boy" is not necessarily intended as an insult but is merely a means of identification; calling somebody "fatty" isn't either as it's not considered bad to be fat in Jamaica. Never give beggars money because doing so only lessens their self-esteem and does nothing to better their situation. The money will soon be gone but their poverty will remain. Begging can be a kind of game or sport for Jamaicans. For example, they may first ask for $5 and then gradually lower the amount until they're only asking for a pittance. They'll keep trying as long as there's a chance of getting something out of you. Be friendly to everybody and it'll soon become evident

which Jamaicans are truly friendly and which only want to get something out of you. Be fair while dealing with locals, but don't let them take advantage of you either. Deal firmly but politely with hustlers; don't let yourself be intimidated. Despite whatever problems you may have with locals, always bear in mind that the vast majority of Caribbean citizens are decent, law-abiding, and struggling to make an honest living. As a foreigner you stick out like a ripe mango on an apple tree, so it's only natural that you will occasionally attract the more unscrupulous type of islander. There's no lack of racial tension on this island, but the level is greatly subdued compared with that of Harlem or Watts. As long as you make a civil attempt at socializing, people will accept you as a person rather than regarding you as a large strolling greenback. If you have time for the locals, they'll always have time for you. You can learn a great deal from the local society just from hanging out. If you're going only for the sun and surf, stay home and use your sun lamp and local swimming pool instead. Jamaica offers such a wealth of experience — tactile, sensual, visual, and oral — that it would be a mistake to ignore it and curl up in a concrete bungalow. Remember that, although you may be spending your vacation in what seems to you a tropical paradise, it's not a paradise for the people living there. Life has always been hard in the Caribbean, and the people have been hard-working and stoic. Don't expect conditions to be as they are in N. America or Europe. They aren't and, owing to the large population relative to the limited resources available, never will be.

WHAT TO TAKE

CHECKLIST

CLOTHING

socks and shoes
underwear
sandals or thongs
T-shirts, shirts (or blouses)
skirts/pants, shorts
swimsuit
hat
light jacket/sweater

TOILETRIES

soap
shampoo
towel, washcloth
toothpaste/toothbrush
comb/brush
prescription medicines
Chapstick/other essential toiletries
insect repellent
suntan lotion/sunscreen
shaving kit
toilet paper
nail clippers
hand lotion
small mirror

OTHER ITEMS

passport
driver's license
travelers cheques
moneybelt
address book
notebook

pens/pencils
books, maps
watch
camera/film
flashlight/batteries
snorkeling equipment
extra glasses
umbrella/poncho
laundry bag
laundry soap/detergent
matches/lighter
frisbee/sports equipment

HIKING & CAMPING

internal frame pack
daypack/shoulder bag
foam sleeping pad
ripstop tape
tent/tent pegs
canteen
first-aid kit
binoculars
compass
hiking shorts/pants
candles/candle lantern
pocket knife
nylon cord
utensils
camping stove
can opener
food containers
spices, condiments
scrubbing pads
pots, pans
plastic wrap/aluminum foil

WHAT TO TAKE

Bring only what's necessary. What you bring will depend upon the length of your stay as well as where you'll go. If you're planning on doing an extensive amount of hiking for example, it'd be a good idea to bring hiking boots, but they're an encumbrance otherwise. Obviously, the camper will have a more voluminous pack than someone who is content to hang around the beach. The lighter you can travel the better. With a light pack, you can breeze from one town to another in the course of a single day. For non-campers, the ideal way to travel is with carry-on luggage such as a day pack. It's possible to leave stuff at the airport, but it's a long way to go back to in case you've forgotten something. It's best to bring everything you think you need—especially a good supply of toiletries, clothing, prescription medicine, and reading material. An internal frame pack is the most convenient for carrying your stuff around in. Try to avoid those with exterior pockets; a lock, though it will not prevent serious theft, will serve as a deterrent to pilfering. A moneybelt, worn around the waist, under your clothes, will keep your money and documents safe.

necessities: Passport and/or other forms of identification, US$ cash, travelers cheques, International Certificate of Vaccination (smallpox—though in practice no one ever checks), International Driving Permit, address book, prescriptions, lock, flashlight (1.5 V batteries), powdered soap, toiletries, sleeping bag or sheet, equipment for camping and food preparation.

useful things to bring: Scotch tape, glue, sewing kit, toilet paper, aspirin, suntan lotion, mask (plus snorkel and fins), rubber thongs, swimming trunks, hiking shorts, rain jacket or poncho, umbrella, compass, etc.

THE NORTH COAST

Perhaps the most legendary stretch of land in the entire Caribbean, considered by many the most beautiful coastline in the world, Jamaica's N coast is famous for its clear waters and fine sand. Enormously rich in its variety of sealife, the long coral reef just off the coast breaks up violent waves and keeps all but the most determined barracuda and sharks at bay. Although a cornucopia of bleak concrete hotels has sprung up along the peripheries of Montego Bay and Ocho Rios, much of the coast remains unexploited. Towns like Falmouth, redolent of past glories, are connected to chic resorts like Ocho Rios and Montego Bay by a smooth highway which passes fragrant flowering trees with yellow blossoms, pasturelands, and rolling, palm-covered hills.

MONTEGO BAY

Most famous of all Jamaica's tourist resorts, Montego Bay—despite its reputation as a high-priced tourist resort town—has much to offer the traveler. The city is divided sharply into two sectors, touristic and residential. The latter area begins with Sam Sharpe Square and continues down Saint James St.; its perpendicular tributaries before Saint James St. merge with Barnett St. and the funkier part of town. Nothing spectacular at all here, but it's pleasant compared with the resort area which begins just the other side of Sam Sharpe Square—here, it's Hustler City. A burro carrying baskets filled with wilting flowers stands under a cluster of hanging baskets; photos can be taken for a suitable fee. Men wearing

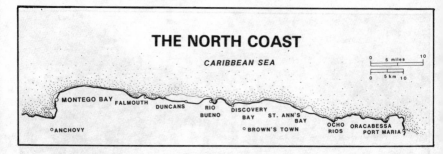

THE NORTH COAST

CARIBBEAN SEA

0 — 5 miles — 10

0 — 5 km — 10

MONTEGO BAY · FALMOUTH · DUNCANS · RIO BUENO · DISCOVERY BAY · ST. ANN'S BAY · OCHO RIOS · ORACABESSA · PORT MARIA

○ANCHOVY · ○BROWN'S TOWN

Rasta caps and a woman wearing a Royal Rent-A-Car ski cap sell souvenirs. This kind of thing continues all the way along the tourist treadway to Doctor's Cay and Cornwall Beach. The remainder of the concrete and glass tourist universe is scattered along the coast outside of town.

arriving by air: If you're on the twice-weekly flight from Port-au-Prince, your plane will be disinfected twice before you will be permitted to leave the aircraft. Immigration and Customs should be speedy, unless you've neglected to buy an onward ticket (in which case you'll be detained for a few hours until someone "soon come" from Air Jamaica to sell you one). Before dealing with the bureaucracy, have a free rum drink, courtesy of Lucky, at his booth. It'll tide you through nicely. A tourist board booth is located next to Lucky's stand, and the foreign exchange booth is located to the rear of the Immigration desks. Walking out of the airport, keep to the R until you reach the marked bus stop (J$0.60 to town). The bus runs from early until late so ignore hustling, rip-off taxi drivers. If you don't have much luggage, it's a pleasant 20-30 min. walk. **getting around:** No place is too far to walk to. Local buses go out to Rose Hall and other destinations.

history: When Columbus was cruising the Caribbean and discovering things for the second time, he anchored at the port now known as Montego Bay. Here, an Arawak volunteer joined his crew. Upon departure, the wind blew well toward Cuba so Columbus, accordingly, named Montego Bay *El Golfo de Buen Tiempo* (Fair Weather Gulf). It was not until 1655 that Montego Bay was noted on Spanish maps as *Manterias*. The name Montego derives from *manteca*, the Spanish word for butter or lard—Spanish settlers once used the bay to ship pig and cattle fat, popularly known as hog's butter. The Parish of St. James was formed by the British in 1665. A 1711 description related that it had no towns, little commerce, and few inhabitants. Because the presence of Maroons and pirates deterred settlers, Montego Bay didn't really take off as a settlement until the last half of the 18th century. During the winter of 1831-32 the town was involved in Jamaica's most serious slave rebellion. It began at Kensington Estate, a few miles inland, and ended with a million pounds in property damage, along with the court-martial and execution of Sam Sharpe and 500 of his followers. A member of the anti-slavery Baptists, Sharpe planned a three-day sit-down strike to take place just after Christmas. Ironically, his plans were circumvented when some of his followers broke into a rum store on the estate, and after getting plastered, set fire to buildings and cane fields. Serving as a signal for slaves on other estates, the red glow of flames spread to nearby hills. Although Sharpe was executed, his revolt forced a reconsideration of slavery, and the British Parliament moved to abolish the practice throughout the British Empire in 1834.

Sam Sharpe

sights: Truthfully, there's not a great deal to see in Montego Bay. The main thing to do is walk through the streets and savor the atmosphere. While you're at it, you might consider stopping in at a few places. More noteworthy for its history than its appearance is Fort Frederick, which overlooks the inner harbor area. In 1760, a gunner, setting off a volley in celebration of the surrender of Havana, had a cannon blow up in his face. In 1795, the fort fired several volleys at the English schooner *Mercury*, mistak-

ing it for a French privateer. Presently, the place is used as a lover's lane at night: great place to bring your girlfriend or boyfriend. The Cage, the stone structure in Sam Sharpe Square, was used to confine runaway slaves, disorderly drunks, and other vagrants. Since then it's been used as a latrine for government employees, a TB clinic, travel agency, and as a RR tour booking office. At the corner of Creek and Dome streets, the Dome, once the only reliable source of water, and now in a state of abject disrepair, was built in 1837. An official called the "Keeper of the Keys" lived, for many years, on the upper floor. Saint James Parish Church, constructed during 1775-82, was damaged by the very severe tremors of the 1957 earthquake and then rebuilt. A relic from an era of bygone affluence, its gardenlike churchyard contains the ostentatious funeral monuments of Jamaican planters—well worth a visit. Resting under the shade of a silk cotton tree, the Slave Ring, located at the corner of East and Union streets, was first used as a slave market and later as a pit for fighting cocks. Brandon Hill Cave, reached by a path located behind the houses at the end of Princess St., has a 25-m-deep rock chamber. The United Fruit Company Wharf, reached by Fish Lane from Barnett St., is the larger of the two banana wharves. See the flurry of activity which accompanies the arrival and departure of a banana boat. The address 12½ King St., is the location of Canterbury, a sprawling squatter settlement in which more than 2,000 humble abodes are crammed onto only a few acres. Quite a contrast to the homes of the ultra-rich set high on the hills above.

beaches: The only free beach in Montego Bay is a small stretch of sand situated next to Walter Fletcher Beach.

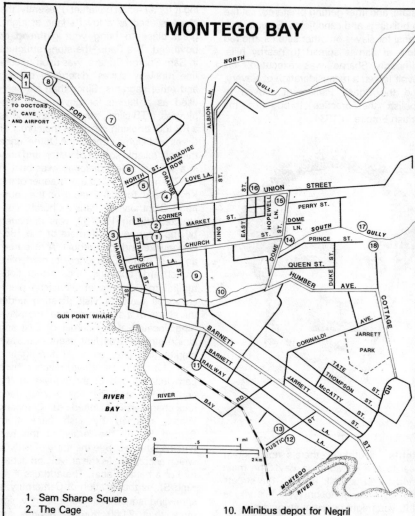

MONTEGO BAY

1. Sam Sharpe Square
2. The Cage
3. Straw Market/Minibus terminal/ bus stop
4. Bay Vista Motel
5. Post Office
6. Parish Library
7. Upstairs Cafe and Macrame Gallery
8. Fort Frederick (Fort Montego)
9. St. James Parish Church
10. Minibus depot for Negril
11. Railway Station
12. Charles Gordon Market
13. I-tal Restaurant
14. Dome House
15. Overton Plaza
16. The Slave Ring
17. Brandon Hill Cave
18. YMCA

Walter Fletcher Beach is now the site of a complex including tennis, netball, and volleyball courts, changing rooms, restaurant, and souvenir shops (open daily, 0830-1700; J$2 admission). Farther up the strip is Doctor's Cave Beach, the most famous beach in all Jamaica. Originally an isolated spot with nothing nearby except tombstones, it was developed and then donated to the town by Dr. Alexander McCatty in 1906. The town rented the beach to a club, and as a result of pressure from the club, in 1929 the town agreed to rent the adjacent Silver Sands Beach. (It was feared that foreign visitors would be driven away if the beach were open to all.) Doctor's Cave was destroyed by the 1932 hurricane, and today, what you see is all you get. Open daily 0830-1700; J$2 admission includes the use of a locker for valuables. Cornwall Beach, across from Casa Montego, is the smallest of all (open daily 0900-1700; J$1 admission).

PRACTICALITIES

accommodations: Needless to say, it's better to arrive here in the off season. Bay Vista Motel, Williams St., has rooms for J$15. Many clubs such as Lyle's Intensified (Barnett St.), MaComba Club (Church Lane), and La Mer (East St.), have accommodations available upstairs. In order to secure a reasonable rate, it's best to tell them you're a Jamaican resident. Mountainside Guesthouse, conveniently located near the airport, corner Federal Ave. and Queen's Dr., charges US$20 s, US$30 d, US$36 t. Nearby are Ocean View and Seville guest houses. Ocean View charges US$22 s, US$34 d, US$39 t; ask for Wayne Matthews. Seville has rooms with a/c for US$25 s, US$40 d, and US$54 t; ask for Wesley Barrett or Easton Powell. Damali Beach Village, three km past the airport to the E, has camping spots for US$5 pp (tents available for hire); ask for Patchi or Arnold. The Montego Bay office of the Jamaican Alternative Hiking and Camping Association is located here as well; open 0900-1700; tel. 952-2387. Four campsites are available at US$5 pp. For extended stays, ask around in town about renting a room. Expect to pay J$10-15 per night with a discount for lengthy stays. (See Chart for additional accommodations.)

food: Avoid tourist restaurants with their astronomical gastronomical prices. Many chain restaurants, like Roadrunner and Kentucky Fried Chicken, are found all over. Best value, however, are the restaurants which line Barnett Street. Capitol Snack, corner Barracks Rd. and Barnett St., has fried fish, delicious codfish and ackee sandwiches, pints of milk, pastries, etc. China Doll Pastry shop, set back behind Sam Sharpe Square, has a large selection of snacks while China Doll Restaurant, Saint James St., has lunchtime specials. Royal Dainties, a Rasta restaurant, is across the street from the General Post Office (G.P.O.). They serve fresh fruit drinks, bean sandwiches (J$2), and rice dishes (J$5). Another, Ital, is across from the Charles Gordon Market. Genuine Rastas turn up frequently at the latter. Rap with them. Upstairs Cafe and Macrame Gallery, at Montego Inn Complex in Fort St., has freshly brewed coffee and a pleasant atmosphere. A German lady runs it. When it's available, Montego Dairies, Church St., has milk and ice cream.

entertainment: One of the best places on the island for nightlife. Plenty of cheap bars line the streets, especially Barnett

MONTEGO BAY ACCOMMODATIONS

HOTEL	ADDRESS	TEL.	HIGH SIN. DBL.		TAX	LOW SIN. DBL.		TAX	SERVICE
Beach View Hotel	Gloucester Ave. (P.O. Box 86)	952-4420 952-4422	30	50	8	30	35	4	10%
Blue Harbour	P.O. Box 212	952-5445	40	46	8	26	32	4	10%
Cariblue Beach Hotel	P.O. Box 210	953-2250	35	40	8	30	40	4	10%
Chalet Caribe	P.O. Box 365	952-1364 952-1635	35	45	8	23	30	4	10%
Coral Cliff Hotel	Gloucester Ave. (P.O. Box 253)	952-4130 952-4131	41	43	10	41	43	6	10%
Hotel Montego	P.O. Box 74	952-3286 952-3287	39	45	8	31	38	4	10%
Ocean View	P.O. Box 210	952-2662	18	28		12	18		10%
Seville Guest House	Sunset Ave.	952-2814 952-1984	25	40		22	40		10%

ROOM RATES AND TAX (US$)

All prices are US$. High season: Dec. 15-April 30. Low season: May 1-Dec. 14. All rates listed are lowest. Higher rates may apply. Accommodation tax applied on a per day, per room basis.

Street. Check signboards and posters to see what's on where. There might be sessions at Del Caso Club, 13A Hart Street. View movie videos for the price of a beer (J$2) at Blue Lagoon on the second floor of City Shopping Centre. See films out under the stars at the Roxy, Barnett St.; a sign by the entrance reads NO RIPE BANANAS ALLOWED. Also try the Strand, Strand St., and the Palladium, Church St., where, on occasion, live talent shows take place. Prostitutes hang out at Sagittarius and Aquarius clubs, and late at night, along the tourist strip. Tourist hangouts include Far Bar (near Doctor's Cave), Pelican, and Winston's. Fantasy Disco is located inside Casa Montego Hotel while Disco Inferno is across the street from Holiday Inn. Jarret Park and Bob Marley Performing Center are the main concert venues.

events and festivals: Reggae Sunsplash, a week-long affair featuring the top names in the music, takes place each Aug. in Jarrett Park. Jonkanoo celebrations are held in the center of town each December. (See "Festivals and Events.")

shopping: A straw market in town caters to tourists, as do the numerous peddlers who line the streets from the General Post Office up through Doctor's Cave and vicinity. As far as shops go, as a general rule of thumb, the farther away from town you get, the higher the prices are. Diane Robertson's book, *Jamaican Herbs,* for example, which sells for J$5.50 at bookstores in town, sells for US$5 at a shop along the tourist strip! If buying from shops or from peddlers, always remember to bargain ferociously.

Prices are bound to be higher during peak season. **Charles Gordon Market:** Located near the end of town on Fustic St.; turn R off Barnett when approaching from the center of town. Vendors spill out of all openings, overflowing up and down the street. At the entrance, men dispense medicines (Zion Searching Herb for worms, etc.) from metal shopping carts. Others sell in front of the VENDORS PROHIBITED sign. Inside, another man, again using a shopping cart, sells ice-cold ginger beer (J$0.80), beet, carrot, and soursop juices. Pandemonium reigns in another area of the packed market as a man wheels a shopping cart filled with freshly baked loaves of bread, a boy runs through shouldering stalks of sugarcane, another struts by selling small packages of dried beans from a basket, and a lady marches through selling shopping bags. The night unveils bingo games, and Kumina and Revival Zion prayer meetings. All of which does not seem to affect in the least the sleep of the female higglers curled up and collapsed in their portion of the octagonal concrete stalls.

services and information: Tourist Information is situated in an attractive complex in front of Cornwall Beach (open Mon. to Fri.; inquire about their Meet the People Program). Banks are located in Sam Sharpe Square. Open Mon. to Thurs. 0900-1400; Fri. 0900-1200, 1400-1700). Change money (US$ and travelers cheques) in tourist shops. Count on getting J$0.30-0.50 or more per dollar above the bank rate. Note that if you change on the street, there's a chance of being ripped off or given counterfeit bills. The G.P.O., located on Saint James St. (open 0900-1630, Mon. to Sat.), has a philatelic bureau. If picking up mail addressed to general delivery, count on a long, agonizing wait. Other post offices are at corner Barnett St. and Cottage Rd. and next to Doctor's Beach. The St. James Parish Library located across from the G.P.O., has a good collection of books on Jamaica in its reference section. Temporary membership cards are available. An American Consulate, complete with a garrulous Reaganite Consul, is located inside the

Revivalist prayer meeting

Blue Harbour Hotel. For those requiring visa extensions, the Immigration Office is located on the third floor of Overton Plaza (open Mon. to Thurs. from 0830-1300, 1400-1700, and on Fri. from 0830-1300, 1400-1600.). The staff here are on a power trip, but as long as you have an onward ticket and are respectful, there should be no problem. Vaughn's Travel Service, 3 Corner Lane off Sam Sharpe Square, gives friendly and accurate service.

TRANSPORT

from Montego Bay: Minibuses leave from Creek St. for Negril and other W and SW destinations. For Ochos Rios, Kingston, and the N coast, minibuses leave from the depot next to the craft market. Slow but full of local color, country buses meander down Barnett Street.

by train: A wonderfully slow, inefficient, but colorful and cheap way to get to Mandeville, Kingston and the more off-the-beaten-track destinations along the way is to board the trains departing daily at 0630 (arrives Kingston 1215) and at 1445 (arrives 2045). For Mandeville, get off in Williamsfield and take a shared taxi. Second-class fare from Montego Bay to Kingston is a very reasonable J$9.10. Turn R at the Esso station on Barracks Rd. and go straight to find the train station.

by air: If you have a Jamaican Airlines ticket going through to Kingston, you'll have to pass through Immigration and Customs upon arrival there so have your passport ready. Trans Jamaican Airlines flies to Kingston, Negril, Ochos Rios, and Port Antonio. For reservations call 952-5401. Flights leave for many international destinations, including Miami, New York City, Port-au-Prince, Grand Cayman, Nassau and Caracas. For San Juan, Puerto Rico, Air Jamaica US$292 excursion fares valid for 17 days allow stopovers in Port-au-Prince and Santo Domingo. Air France, Eastern, and Air Jamaica offer APEX excursion fares to Miami for a mere US$160, and VIASA 10-day excursion fares to Caracas are also a good deal at just US$176. Other 10-day VIASA excursion fares include Aruba, US$110, and Curacao, US$180. For Georgetown, Grand Cayman, Air Jamaica has a US$150 RT fare.

VICINITY OF MONTEGO BAY

heading south: Ms. Lisa Salmon's bird sanctuary is at Rocklands along the road to Anchovy. Tame birds will eat right out of your hand. (Open daily from 1500, J$2 admission.) An antiquated but still functioning water wheel at Tryall stands next to a golf course. Note the date 1834 inscribed along its base which indicates that the works were rebuilt after the 1832 slave rebellion. Perhaps the finest example of sugar estate ruins on the island, the mid-18th C. sugar factory at Kenilworth was constructed with great care. The shell of the H-shaped building stands next to the finely built Georgian water mill. The adjoining youth corps camp, patterned after the Civilian Conservation Corps, is well worth a visit.

heading east: The road in this direction is intermittently lined with hotels. Most famous attraction out this way is Rose Hall Great House. Take a local bus (J$2.80 to get here; keep a sharp lookout for a white sign on the right). Open daily 0900-1800, J$15 or US$5 admission.

Said to be the grandest 18th C. plantation house in the entire W. Indies, it has been restored to its former grandeur by an American millionaire at a cost of US$2.5 million. Although it contains numerous 17th C. antiques and art treasures, most of these have been imported from abroad. There are many legends surrounding Annie Palmer, the "White Witch" of Rose Hall, who allegedly haunts the estate. One claims that she poisoned her first husband before going

through another four. She also took on numerous slaves as lovers, murdering them as she tired of them. Finding her cruelty unbearable, slaves rebelled and murdered her in her bed in 1833. On Fri., 13 Oct. 1978, a crowd of 8,000 turned out to watch a team of psychics attempt to commune with her *duppy*. Bambos, a Greek Cypriot, received a psychic communication which led to the discovery of a huge termite mound containing a brass urn with a voodoo doll interred inside.

FALMOUTH

Best preserved 18th C. town on the island, Falmouth still retains much of the Georgian style, in terms of harmony and symmetry, that it had at its zenith. Despite the valiant efforts of the Georgian Society, buildings continue to deteriorate, and those once roofed with shingles have been replaced with zinc. But the charm of the place is still very much intact. Old ladies still harness their mules in front of shops, goats still wander through the streets munching on shrubbery, and fishermen mend nets by the sea. Best time to visit is mid-afternoon when a sea breeze wafts over the main streets.

history: Founded at the end of the 18th C., the town flourished for less than 50 years before the prosperity of the sugar planters reached its peak. Given its name because Trelawny Parish's first governor was born in Falmouth, England, it became a free port in 1809. Its decline was due, in part, to the rise of Kingston as a commercial center, the increase in the size of ships which could no longer utilize its harbor, and the extension of the railroad to Montego Bay.

sights: Like early Kingston, Falmouth was laid out on a regular plan. Many scenes from the movie "Papillon" were filmed along Main Street. Numerous old buildings are grouped around central Water Square; less extensively renovated, however, are the ones along Market Street. Saint Peter's Church, Duke St., has a magnificent stained glass window. The old courthouse (1815) was remodeled after burning in the 1820s and has never been the same since. William Knibb Presbyterian Church is dedicated to a man who was the most outspoken opponent of slavery on the island; his chapel was dubbed "Knibb's pestilential praying hole." On Emancipation Day in 1834, hundreds of slaves poured into town. At a nighttime ceremony, Knibb, speaking before an assembly at midnight, shouted, "The monster is dead. The Negro is free." As a part of the ceremony the shackles of slavery were buried in a coffin inscribed "Colonial Slavery died July 31, 1834 aged 276 years." **accommodations:** Cheapest and only is Falmouth Resort, Duke St., J$55 s or d.

vicinity of Falmouth: Stewart Castle is a coastal estate a few km E of Falmouth which contains the remains of an unusual fortified house. It is currently the property of the Jamaica National Trust Commission. Windsor Cave to the S, one of the better-known caves on the island, is also one of the largest and most accessible. Many beautiful stalactites and stalagmites. Hampstead Estate contains the ruins of a factory, millpond, water tank, and cattle mill. Good Hope Estate has been lovingly restored. Dating from 1742, the grounds include water wheels, ruins, and a counting house. There are over 300 km of riding trails, and horses can be rented. Reservations by writing Good Hope Estate, c/o Falmouth P.O., Trelawny.

DISCOVERY BAY

Originally known as Puerto Seco (Dry Harbor), the name of this small, largely middle-class community was changed to commemorate the spot where Columbus first landed. Someone made a mistake, however, because · historians contend that he actually landed a few km W at Rio Bueno. The bauxite boom that took place in the '60s brought prosperity to this area, which has become a Jamaican version of American suburbia, complete with private beach and modest sports club. Except for a shopping center, post office and library, there's not much here save peace and quiet—a great place to unwind. A marine coral research center, run by the University of the West Indies, is just out of town along A1 to the west. Farther along the same road is a monstrously ugly bauxite terminal. Far-

ther still is Columbus Park which has a great view and an outdoor museum which includes cannons, a water wheel, and a stone crest.

accommodations and food: Cantankerous Mr. Alexander, down the road from the P.O., offers attractive rooms for J$25 (negotiable) which include use of the communal kitchen. Clean and serene. Spanish Court Apartments (tel. 973-2235/2423) are up on the hill. A swimming pool is outside this former hotel erected during the '60s hotel boom. Completely furnished apartments (complete cooking facilities and utensils, two beds, couch and balcony) rent for J$60 per night or J$360 per week. Negotiate. Other accommodations are listed under Runaway Bay.

North Coast market scene

VICINITY OF DISCOVERY BAY

Rio Bueno: Take a minibus along A1 to the W and cross over Bengal Bridge (1798) and into Trelawny Parish where this miniscule but historic town is situated. Old warehouses, churches and Ft. Dundas here serve as a reminder of colonial times. Once an important port, it's now a quiet fishing village. Parts of the movie "A High Wind in Jamaica" were filmed on the main street. The two attractive churches here are the Rio Bueno Anglican Church (1883) and the Rio Bueno Baptist Church (1901). Fort Dundas (1778), at the end of the harbor, has been largely absorbed by the contiguous schoolyard.

Brown's Town and vicinity: Take the road which heads N from the shopping plaza to Orange Valley Estate. This privately owned, 2,300-acre estate consists of an H-shaped great house, stone slave hospital, and boiling room with its 19th C. boiler added later. Sugar production ceased in these 18th C. buildings only in the middle of the 20th century. Ar-

range tours at the Estate Community Centre. Farther S are the grounds of Minard Estate which contains New Hope and Minard great houses. Centrally located at the junction of four main roads, Brown's Town is named after its founder, Irishman Hamilton Brown. This hilly country market town is home to one of Jamaica's leading artists, Gloria Escoffery. Studio Escoffery (tel. 975-2268) can be visited upon appointment. The market is held here on Sat. under the huge, tin-roofed outdoor market. Farther S near Alexandria is the "village" of Nine Miles, where Rastafarian reggae saint Bob Marley was born and lies buried. Decorated with flowers and pictures of Haile Selassie, his tomb is enshrined in a chapel atop a hillside. All-night memorial birthday concerts are held at this spot every February.

heading east: Contrary to popular opinion, the people who ran away from what's now the resort area of Runaway Bay (whence its name), were African slaves fleeing to Cuba, not Spanish fleeing from the British. Touristic Runaway Caves and Green Grotto are in this area. Although most of the accommodations

interior of a boiling house as shown in a 19th C. print

are ultra-expensive, Bell's at Salem to the E has s or d rooms for J$60 including private bath and use of shared living room and kitchen. Ask for Mrs. Stephenson at the house next door. Farther back on the road in the direction of Runaway is North Drive which charges J$50 for rooms. Farther E, near the Columbus Monument and Seville great house, are the ruins of Sevilla La Nueva, abandoned after the Spanish left for the greener pastures of Spanish Town in 1534 — just 24 years after its founding. Nothing remains of the original settlement save archaeological ruins which are being excavated with the goal of establishing a major cultural and historical center here in time for the 500th anniversary in 1992 of Columbus's first voyage. A search is currently underway for Columbus's two caravals which were beached and abandoned here in 1503-04. Capital of St. Ann's Parish, the village (pop. 8,000) of St. Ann's is just a bit farther down the road. Besides being the birthplace of national hero Marcus Garvey, it is notable for its historic courthouse (1860) and fort. Used until recently as a slaughterhouse, St. Ann's Bay Fort was built in 1750 of stone blocks hauled from the ruins of Sevilla La Nueva. A scene from the film "Dr No" was shot at Cotter's Wharf. Due S of St. Ann, at Pedro between Claremont and Kellits, stand the ruins of the small storied house equipped with circular towers, known as Edinburgh Castle. Here lived the "mad doctor" Lewis Hutchinson, the infamous 18th C mass murderer. Perhaps as many as 40 travelers over the years were shot, robbed, and decapitated while his slaves

caravels of Columbus: On 25 June 1503, on Columbus's fourth and final voyage, he was marooned for one year at "Santa Gloria" (now St. Ann's Bay). His leaking, worm-eaten ships — the Capitano and the Santiago — were beached here. A search is now underway to locate them.

stood silent witness. Discovered after he shot a neighbor, Hutchinson was captured while attempting to flee by ship. Before being hanged in Spanish Town in 1773, he willed 100 pounds for the construction of a monument whose epitaph would have read: "Their sentence, pride, and power I defy. Despise their power, and like a Roman I die." Needless to say, it was never erected.

OCHO RIOS

Unlike other N coast towns, which have regressed from bustling ports into quiet fishing villages, Ocho Rios has done just the opposite, metamorphosing from a sleepy fishing village into a bustling tourism and bauxite shipping center. If you're in search of unspoiled Jamaica, you won't find it here. Unlike Montego Bay, Ocho Rios is a planned tourist resort. The government-owned St. Ann Development Company acquired land in the Ochos Rios area during the 1960s, dredged the harbor, and reclaimed the white sand beach. The name Ocho Rios is a corruption of the Spanish word *chorreros* ("waterfall"); the Spanish gave this stretch of coastline the name because of the large number of waterfalls (now mostly tapped for hydroelectricity) which line this coast.

getting there: Direct minibuses run from Montego Bay and Kingston. From Port Antonio it's necessary to change several times. It's also possible to fly into Ochos Rios airport directly from New York or Miami.

sights: Ochos Rios Fort stands outside of town to the W next to Reynold's bauxite installation. Recently rebuilt by Reynold's Jamaica, the late 17th C. fort contains two original cannon and two borrowed from Mammee Bay. One of the most famous and popular attractions in Jamaica, Dunn's River Falls are on a paved road off to the south. Open 0900-1800, there's a J$2 entrance fee with an additional J$1 charge to climb the falls. Guides depend upon tips for their income. Your guide will help you climb and carry your gear as you slip and slide all along the way to the top of this gently sloping waterfall. A bathing beach, snack bar, and toilets are located at its base where the water tumbles into the ocean. The battle of Los Chorreros was fought near this spot, in which the English defeated the Spanish Expeditionary Force from Cuba. Much more private and less frequented is the waterfall one mile farther W at the hydroelectric station.

practicalities: Not a great deal of cheap

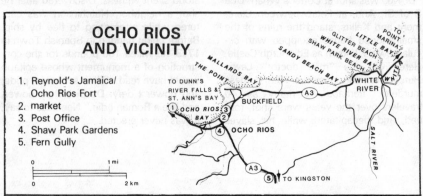

OCHO RIOS AND VICINITY

1. Reynold's Jamaica/ Ocho Rios Fort
2. market
3. Post Office
4. Shaw Park Gardens
5. Fern Gully

0   1 mi

0   2 km

Dunn's River Falls

accommodations are available here. Ask around and bargain at the few small guest houses that exist. If camping, see George Barnes at Milford Falls about pitching a tent. He has 15 tent spaces and charges US$5 pp per night. Friendship Farm Camp, 11 km (seven miles) S of Ocho Rios near Hopewell and Orange Hall, has 12 buses which have been converted into cabins in the middle of a 600-acre farm nestled in the hills at 500 m (1600 feet). Doubles are US$15 and rooms for four are US$30. Many small restaurants line the streets of Ocho Rios. Discos and music spots include The Ruins, which has live bands, and Decade Disco. A tourist board office is located inside Pineapple Place.

VICINITY OF OCHO RIOS

To the S along A3 just outside of town are the ornately landscaped Shaw Park Gardens. A bit farther is Fern Gully. Of obscure origin but thought to have been planned out by a Superintendent of Public Gardens in the 1880s, vegetation has been decimated several times since

then by floods and hurricanes. Six and a half km (four miles) to the E stands Harmony Hall, an old house (1896) which has been transformed into an art gallery, craft center and pub-restaurant. Prospect Plantation, near Oracabessa, offers a variety of tours (tel. 974-0253). Near Oracabessa is Firefly, Noel Coward's home. Difficult to reach on a 305-m-high plateau, it has been immaculately preserved and transformed into a museum. Longtime housekeeper Imogene Frazier now acts as a tourguide. Preserved almost as he left it, the interior contains his paintings, two pianos, writing desk, and other such memorabilia. Closed Tues. and Thursday. A short distance down the road is Golden Eye, the home of Ian Fleming. Here he wrote many of his famous James Bond novels. The house is closed to the public.

Port Maria: Capital of St. Mary's Parish, this small town, stretched out along two bays strewn with huge rocks which separate them, was once a bustling banana port. The sign reading TO THE TACKY MONUMENT, does not, as the name suggests, lead to a tacky, tasteless monument but rather to one dedicated to

Jamaican freedom fighter Tacky who led a slave insurrection in 1760. This rebellion, brutally put down by the authorities, was led by "Coromantees" or slaves from Ghana's Asante warrior tribe. Ruins of Ft. Haldane stand near Gray's Charity at the edge of town. Mannings Hotel has rooms with common bath. Camping and rooms are available at Dream Beach and Sea Lawn Coral Beach. Frontier is an old estate at the E end of the bay which is where Tacky's revolt originated.

Strawberry Fields: Truly off the beaten track, Strawberry Fields offers a distinctly different Jamaican experience. The location is incredibly beautiful: waves crash onto coral outcrops in front of the mountains rising in the distance. On the other side is a small, sheltered white sand beach. Goats manicure the grass between the cabins. Full moon nights are exquisite, and the local community is hospitable. To get here turn N by the sign on the road between Annotto Bay and Port Maria. Walk three km to Robin's Bay and then one and a half km to the campground. No public transportation so try hitching. Strawberry Fields campground has very pricey tents (US$22 s, US$40 d) and even more expensive cottages. Breakfast is included in these prices, but the government accommodation tax is not. The solution is to bring your own tent. Camping is US$5 per night; negotiate for longer stays. Toilets and showers are provided but not cooking facilities. Locals living in the vicinity also rent huts (from J$10 per day and up). Eat up the road at the second of two food stalls from the gate.

AROUND THE
EAST COAST

PORT ANTONIO

A small town perched above two natural harbors, Port Antonio is perhaps the most beautiful settlement in all Jamaica: the location and setting couldn't be more perfect. The surrounding Portland Parish scenery is magnificent with white sand beaches and small, classic islands just off the shoreline. The town itself is compact without being claustrophobic. Its easygoing atmosphere contrasts dramatically with the island's other resort towns. **getting there:** Take any bus or minibus from Kingston or Annotto Bay. No through minibuses leave from Ocho Rios so you must change along the way. If planning to go straight through from Montego Bay, leave early.

history: Although the first British settlers attempted to change the name to Titchfield, the original name of the small Spanish settlement, Puerto Anton, prevailed in the end. In order for the British to maintain their grip on this corner of the island where slaves far outnumbered overseers, land grants were offered to settlers from Europe, and the town was laid out. To protect the settlers, Fort George was constructed on Titchfield peninsula, and Navy Island was renamed and fortified. Bananas, from the Canary Islands introduced to Jamaica by way of Hispaniola by the Spaniards, were scorned as being food fit only for animals. It never occurred to the Jamaicans to export them, until entrepreneur Capt. Lorenzo Dow Baker discovered the profit in shipping to New England when he made US$2000 delivering an unripened boatload in 1871. Baker

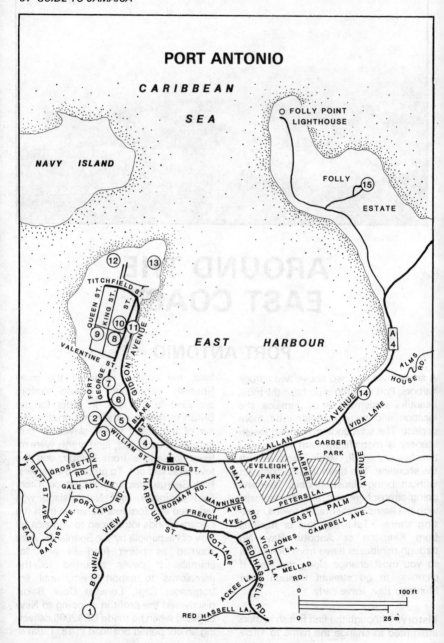

PORT ANTONIO

CARIBBEAN

SEA

FOLLY POINT
LIGHTHOUSE

NAVY ISLAND

FOLLY
ESTATE

(15)

(12)   (13)

TITCHFIELD ST.

QUEEN ST.
KING ST.

(10)
(9)   (8)   (11)

VALENTINE ST.

EAST   HARBOUR

FORT GEORGE ST.

GIDEON AVENUE

(7)

(6)

(2)   (5)

(3)   (4)   BLAKE ST.

WILLIAM ST.

BRIDGE ST.

A4

ALMS HOUSE RD.

AVENUE

(14)   VIDA LANE

ALLAN

HARPER LA.

CARDER PARK

EVELEIGH PARK

PETERS LA.

EAST   PALM   AVENUE

CAMPBELL AVE.

SMATT RD.

MANNINGS AVE.

NORMAN RD.

FRENCH AVE.

VICTOR LA.

JONES LA.

MELLAD RD.

RED HASSELL RD.

COTTAGE

ACKEE LA.

RED HASSELL LA.

HARBOUR ST.

BONNIE VIEW RD.

PORTLAND RD.

GALE RD.

GROSSETT RD.

LOVE LANE

BAPTIST AVE.

W. BAPT ST. AVE.

EAST

(1)

0   100 ft

0   25 m

started and built up the Boston Fruit Company, which merged with the United Fruit Company in 1939. The U.F.C. monopoly lasted for a few years thereafter, until it was broken, partly by the effects of Panama Disease on the banana crop and partly by competition from the newly formed Jamaica Banana Producer's Association. Since then, exports have shifted toward Britain and quantities have declined. One day in 1947, Errol Flynn, sailing in on his yacht *Zacca,* discovered the town and decided to make it his home. Moving quickly, he purchased the Titchfield Hotel (which he renamed the Jamaica Reef), and Navy I. just off the coast. Largely because of his presence, Port Antonio became the "in" place for the rich and powerful in the 1950s. Some of this glamour remains today in the form of the villas which line the roads around the Blue Hole.

SIGHTS

Best way to get oriented is to take the steep road up Richmond Hill to the Bon-

nie View Hotel which commands a perfect view of the bay below. Magnificent place to watch sunsets. From the center of town follow Fort Saint George St. to the end and turn L to find the ruins of Errol Flynn's Jamaica Reef Hotel. A path to the L leads to a small beach. What was once the exclusive property of the rich is now—thanks to a fire—the property of all. A pleasant spot to sit and meditate. Hurry and get here before some developer moves in and builds again. Look for banana boats departing from here. What little remains of Fort St. George has been built into the Titchfield School at the same end of the peninsula. At the other end of town, just on the L side of the road heading E, turn L on a side road marked by two empty sentry boxes and a JAMAICA FOR JESUS sign. Follow this road up and enter Folly Estate. In 1905 Alfred Mitchell from New London, Connecticut, had this mansion built, but his wife refused to live in it. He lived here off and on until he died in 1912. In 1938 the roof fell in because the iron reinforcement rods had been corroded by sea salt. Acquired by the government in 1949, it was leased to Mrs. Errol Flynn for construction of a resort, but this project fell through. And so it remains today—a ruined concrete and limestone mansion with a winding staircase to the top, sexually explicit graffiti scrawled on the side, and Doric pillars cast from concrete. From the beach below swim or wade over to Wood Island just offshore. Despite the name, there are but two palms and a few other trees for shade. The roof of this mansion would be a perfect place to take in the full moon or stargaze. Other buildings are scattered over the plain with a few in front of the entrance to the small red-and-white striped lighthouse. Back out on the road, take a bus or hitch to Folly II. Although

PORT ANTONIO

1. Bonnie View Hotel
2. bus station
3. market
4. Hope View Guest House
5. Dragon Plaza (Front Porch Restaurant, Tourist Information)
6. Court House/Post Office
7. Delmar Theater
8. DeMontevin Guest House
9. Scotia Guest House
10. Rose's Restaurant
11. Ms. Peggy's Place
12. Jamaica Reef Beach
13. Titchfield School
14. Stop Brap Restaurant
15. Folly Ruins

Ruins of Folly I

construction was abandoned in 1980, this concrete structure, with its gaping windows and rising turrets, appears to be a Bavarian medieval castle when viewed from a distance. The German baroness who ordered its construction ran into problems when she was caught smuggling funds out of the country illegally. To one side of the "castle," rough coral bluffs engage in combat with the sea as the waves clash and recede. Definitely a location to visit when it's thundering and a storm is brewing. A few km farther down the road is San San Beach (J$2 admission), one of the prettiest beaches on the N coast. This white sand beach is almost deserted on weekdays, even in peak season. Monkey Island (also known as Pellew I.) is visible from the shore of San San. Covered with colorful vegetation, it no longer has any monkeys.

Blue Hole and beyond: The legendary Blue Lagoon or Blue Hole is farther down the road past Monkey Island. Turn L off the main road and follow the sloping, flower-wreathed road leading to it. Quiet and serene, this beautiful spot is composed of a mixture of salt- and freshwater released from underground streams. Dropping off sharply from near the shoreline, the bottom plummets to a depth of 65 m (210 ft.), which accounts for its intense, emerald-green clarity. A jungle path surrounds the sides of the lagoon. Bring your own lunch and some bread for feeding the fish. The entire area surrounding the Blue Lagoon contains the island's most deluxe hotels and villas; Trident, Frenchman's Cove and Jamaica Hill are among those which charge US$200 per night with two meals. Boston Beach, a small but beautiful beach set between towering cliffs, is farther down the road. The area around this beach is famous all over Jamaica for its jerk pork. Locals here learned to make it from the Maroons. Still farther is the less frequented and more spacious Long Bay, with its immaculate beach. Back in town, access to privately owned, lush and resplendent Navy I. can be obtained by phoning Mr. Casey at 993-2667. Not much here except a beach or two, but the privacy is complete.

PRACTICALITIES

accommodations: Cheapest but with only three rooms is The Rose at J$15 pp. De Montevin Lodge next door is much more expensive, and it's necessary to pay hotel tax. Still, at US$11 and up pp, it's not too bad. A favorite with travelers is Scotia Guest House, just around the corner. The price depends upon the number of people and length of stay. Hopeview Guest House, conveniently located on Harbour St., has friendly management and rooms from J$25. Rooms above the Sunset Bar go for J$20 s and J$30 d. Way Valley Guesthouse, 11 West Palm Ave., has rooms from J$20. Pleasant, airy rooms with meals available upon request.

food: Best deal in town is Ms. Peggie's place in an unmarked building across from The Rose. About J$6-7 for sump-tuous and delicious meals. Cheapest place in town is Cool Runnings, Ltd. where goat's head soup is only J$1.20, brown stewed fish J$4.50. The Ice Cream Parlour and Snack next to Delmar Theater has friendly local atmosphere. Also try Black Gold on Blake Street. Stop Brap, at the edge of town on the way to Folly Estate, has jerk chicken at J$12/lb. and roast fish at J$10/lb. For a splurge, try the De Montevin or Bonnie View Hotel. Front Porch Restaurant in Dragon Plaza is virtually the only place serving on Sunday.

entertainment: Innumerable bars line the streets, but the action's at City Club on West St., with canned reggae and dancing every night. Inside a line of Rastas, their locks fashionably secured under large felt caps, move hands and beer bottles up and down, jiving in time to the music. Also try the Blue Jay Club on the edge of town. The sole movie theater, the Delmar, is on Harbour Street.
shopping: Not much to buy here. Check out the food market on Thurs. and Saturday. Boatyard Graphics, showroom for a handicapped workshop, has some nice

jerk pork: An island special-ty, this method of spicing and grilling pork originated with the Portland Parish Maroons who relied on wild hogs for survival. Today, the best jerk pork on the island is still said to be made in Portland Parish.

things. Located at 55A West Palm Avenue. **services and information:** A small Tourist Board office is located in Dragon Plaza. A branch of the Jamaica Information Service is in the rear of a building on the other side of the street. The library is set back on Harbour Street.

from Port Antonio: Minibuses and buses leave from the area around the market for Ocho Rios, Moore Town and other destinations. Be aware that there are two routes to Kingston: one through Morant Bay and one via Buff Bay.

VICINITY OF PORT ANTONIO

Jamaica's spectacular E coast runs from Port Antonio past Boston and Long bays. If intent upon staying along this coast, ask around for accommodation. Cliff View/Ross Craig near Devil's Elbow has camping for US$3 pp per night and two

rooms available at US$5 pp. A few km E of Boston Bay lies the ranch of Mrs. Errol Flynn, where she resides along with 2,000 head of cattle. Reach Falls, small, exquisite, and relatively untouristed, has been acclaimed as the most beautiful spot in Jamaica. Turn R one and a half km (one mile) after Machioneal and follow the rough road for three km (two miles) until you come to a fork which leads there. A group of self-appointed maintenance men will try to hit you for a fee. Pay if you like.

heading west: Rafting trips on the Rio Grande, a touristic diversion, leave from Rafter's Rest. For the best price, bargain with the raftsmen who hang out on Harbour St. across from the post office. Eleven km (seven miles) W is Somerset Falls. A lush garden surrounds the lower falls; the larger one lies at the end of a narrow gorge accessible by swimming or raft. Admission is J$2 which includes the

Port Antonio Court House

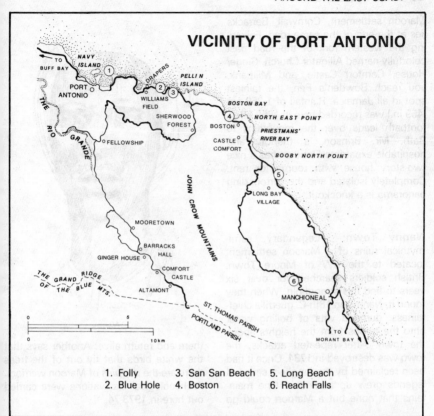

VICINITY OF PORT ANTONIO

TO BUFF BAY

NAVY ISLAND

PORT ANTONIO

THE RIO GRANDE

DRAPERS

WILLIAMS FIELD

SHERWOOD FOREST

PELLIN ISLAND

FELLOWSHIP

BOSTON BAY

BOSTON

NORTH EAST POINT

CASTLE COMFORT

PRIESTMANS' RIVER BAY

BOOBY NORTH POINT

JOHN CROW MOUNTAINS

LONG BAY VILLAGE

MOORETOWN

BARRACKS HALL

GINGER HOUSE

COMFORT CASTLE

ALTAMONT

THE GRAND RIDGE OF THE BLUE MTS.

MANCHIONEAL

ST. THOMAS PARISH
PORTLAND PARISH

TO MORANT BAY

0 ___ 5
0 ___ 10km

1. Folly
2. Blue Hole
3. San San Beach
4. Boston
5. Long Beach
6. Reach Falls

raft trip. It's only J$1 if you swim back (much more fun), but you'll have to bargain with the person in charge. **accommodations:** Rio-Sol-Mar, near Hope Bay, has rooms for US$15 and campsites at US$3.50 pp. Fish Dome, located on the road heading S past Chepstrow, has a large cabin available at US$10 pp. Camping is also available at US$5 pp.

heading south: The area surrounding the Jim Crow Mountains and the Blue Mountains, which they abut, is one of the most picturesque areas of Jamaica.

Unlike the side facing Kingston, the mountains here receive incredible amounts of rainfall and are virtually untouched. Lush and spectacular vegetation and views abound. Moore Town, the home of the Windward Maroons, lies on the eastern fork of the road running S from Port Antonio. Fronted by a graveyard, the Anglican Church, oldest building in town, is to the L as you enter. Across from the school, Bump Grave contains the remains of the national heroine Nanny, a Maroon leader who was a legendary fighter. Note the Maroon flag flying next to the Jamaican. Another

Maroon settlement, Cornwall Barracks lies at the end of the same road. Following the western fork of the road past colorfully-named Alligator Church, Ginger House, Comfort Castle, and Millbank, you reach Bowden's Pen, the rainiest spot in all Jamaica. Rainfall of 1,259 cm (459 in.) was recorded here in 1959-60. A footpath leads over the mountains to Bath. Mr. Brinson, a friendly and hospitable expatriate Floridian has a nice two-story house with rooms for rent. Completely isolated and the surrounding panorama is a knockout.

Nanny Town: Legendary, semi-mythical ruins of a Maroon settlement located to the SW of Moore Town. British soldiers searched for over six years to find this stronghold. When they found it, Nanny, an 18th-C. guerrilla chieftainess, dumped vats of boiling water onto the troops from the heights above the town. After repeated attacks, the town was destroyed in 1734. Once it had been reclaimed by the jungle, a series of legends grew up around it. One maintains that none but a Maroon could go

Nanny

there and return alive. Another says that the white birds that fly out of the trees there are the *duppies* of Maroon warriors. Archaeological excavations were carried out here in 1973-74.

BATH

A small farming community, Bath is noted for its hotsprings and Botanical Garden. Officially named The Bath of St. Thomas the Apostle, the spring was discovered by a runaway slave in the 1690s. Discovering that the warm waters of a forest pool cured tropical ulcers on his legs, he returned to tell his owner about his miraculous discovery. The government bought the spring in 1699, and a town was promoted by a public corporation. Soon it became the most fashionable spot on the island. Political clashes during the late 1600s caused

Bath to lose its fashionable image; it soon became a ghost town with only 10 inhabitants. Today, only the baths and the Botanical Gardens remain to attest to its former glory. The springs are unique because the water issues both hot and cold. The water, high in lime and sulfur, is regarded as being especially valuable in treating skin diseases and rheumatic ailments. Buy a ticket (J$2) and bathe in one of the tanks inside the hotel, or take a hike up behind the hotel and bathe in the water flowing from an overhead bamboo pipe. While the hotel is set back at the end of a road leading from town, the Botanical Gardens are right in the center of town. Now a mere shadow of their former splendor, these are the second oldest gardens in the Western Hemisphere. Many of the plants and trees first introduced to Jamaica were planted here, including the original breadfruit trees brought over by Captain Bligh. The descendants of these trees may still be seen in one corner of the garden.

accommodations and food: Bath Fountain Hotel (tel. 982-2632/2315) has rooms from J$30 s and J$40 d (plus hotel tax and 10 percent service charge). Use of the bath is included in the price. Although it's a bit rundown and deteriorating, it still retains its own special charm. Meals range in price from J$8 at breakfast to J$14 for dinner. There's also a small restaurant in the town itself. Avoid this hotel on weekends when Kingstonites arrive in hordes.

from Bath: A path leads over the Blue Mountains from Hayfield to Bowden Pen. Most frequent transport is to and from Morant Bay. Transport to Hordley near the E coast is available but very infrequent. Count on walking unless you get lucky and hitch a ride.

MORANT BAY

Capital of St. Thomas Parish, this tiny town is of note chiefly for its historic associations with the Morant Bay Rebellion, which took place in 1865, led by Baptist deacon Paul Bogle. When Bogle, along with 400 followers, marched on Morant Bay Court House on 11 October to present their grievances, they clashed with the local volunteer militia. During the ensuing melee, the courthouse, seen as a symbol of injustice, was burned to the ground and many prominent citizens were murdered. Declaring martial law, the governor unleashed the soldiers on the local populace. Soldiers torched 1,000 homes and executed after courtsmartial more than 430 women and men. Using the uprising as an excuse to rid himself of a vociferous spokesman for the poor in the legislature, the governor had George Gordon brought to Morant Bay and, after framing him with responsibility for the uprising, ordered him hung in front of the charred ruins of the courthouse. Bogle suffered the same fate. As an aftermath of the controversy surrounding the handling of the uprising, the governor was recalled and Jamaica became a Crown Colony. The powerful and dynamic statue of Paul Bogle, sculpted by Edna Manley, stands in front of the rebuilt courthouse. During excavations in 1975, a total of 79 skeletons were found inside old refuse dumps located inside Morant Bay Fort.

vicinity of Morant Bay: Yallahs Ponds, nearby to the S of the highway, have

Paul Bogle statue

twice the salinity of seawater due to evaporation. The early settlers obtained their salt here. The ruins of a small stone signal tower found here are listed as a National Monument. Judgment Cliff is a 1,600-m (1,000-ft.) escarpment visible from the Yallahs River. This is the only tangible reminder of the 1692 earthquake which sank Port Royal. According to local legend, it received its name when the landslide buried the plantation of a Dutchman who maltreated his slaves. Best view is from Easington. Cane River Falls can be reached from Bull Bay. Nearest accommodation is Joe Corniffe's Gold Mine Club and Camp located at Green Wall to the W along the main highway to Kingston. Joe charges US$5

pp for rooms and US$2 pp to camp. Heading E along A4 from Morant Bay are the once-busy banana and sugar ports of Port Morant and Bowden. At one time guarded by Fort Lindsay on one side and Fort William on the other, Point Morant still has two fine beaches: Lyssons and Roselle. Between Bowden and the sea lies a low flat triangle of land known as Holland. Said to have been the most prosperous sugar plantation in Jamaica, it was owned by Simon Taylor, the wealthiest man in the W. Indies in his day. Just off the highway near Golden Grove lie the remains of Stokes Hall, one of the oldest holdings in Jamaica. Morant Bay Lighthouse is set between Quaco and South East Point.

KINGSTON

INTRODUCTION

A city of contrasts, Kingston is the capital and also the largest (pop. 850,000) English-speaking city S of Miami. Not only is the island's most expensive architecture found here, but the worst poverty as well. Old Georgian buildings and soaring skyscrapers contrast vividly with the JLP and PNP graffiti that demarcate political zones in Kingston's turbulent slums. "Kings-town hot-to" goes the reggae song, implying the city's underlying social stresses. In this economically and politically polarized city, tension lies pulsating just under the surface. Sometimes it explodes and results in shootings and gang wars in W. Kingston. Kingston, however, is a much safer city to visit than New York or Miami. From the harbor, Kingston spreads out across the fan-shaped Liguanea Plains to the first slopes of the Blue Mountains. Downtown Kingston is a quiet collection of streets which still retain a bit of charm. New Kingston, a plastic city-within-a-city containing the edifices of the multinationals and banks, is the hub of business operations in Jamaica. Halfway Tree and Cross Roads are the major reference and transportation transfer points.

history: Kingston started out as Colonel Barry's Hog Crawle in the 1600s. After Port Royal was devastated during the 1692 earthquake, survivors flocked to Kingston. Land was purchased, and the streets were laid out on a grid pattern which remains intact to this day. In 1802 Kingston was chartered as a Corporation with Mayor and Council; it became the capital in 1872. The 1907 earthquake and fire destroyed many of the old buildings downtown. Since 1960, a major effort has been underway to revitalize this area through renovation and construction.

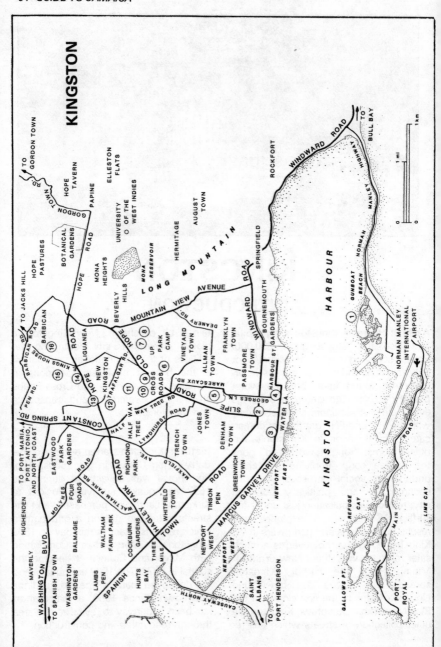

KINGSTON AND LOWER ST. ANDREW

1. Palisadoes Park
2. Parade
3. Railway Station
4. Institute of Jamaica
5. National Heroes Park
6. Little Theater and Public Archives
7. National Arena
8. National Stadium
9. USIS
10. Pegasus Hotel
11. Jamaica Tourist Board
12. Mrs. Johnson, Mrs. Derry, Indies House
13. Devon House
14. Jamaica House
15. Kings House
16. Sandhurst

getting there: Minibuses run regularly from Montego Bay, Ocho Rios, Mandeville, and Port Antonio. There's also slow but inexpensive train service between Montego Bay, Williamsfield (Mandeville), and Kingston. **arriving by air:** Outside the airport, fend off hustling taxi drivers and take an X97 minibus (J$1.50) to W. Parade. It leaves every half hour until 2200 and takes 30 min. to cover the 18 km (11 miles). If headed for New Kingston, get off at the base of Mountain View Ave. and transfer to a Halfway Tree-bound minibus. If proceeding to Jack's Hill, take a No. 54 bus to Barbicon and then hitch or take a bus up to the top of Jack's Hill Road.

getting around: After the heavily in-debted city bus service was abandoned in 1984, routes were franchised out to privately owned minibuses. Charges are by zone and run from J$0.60 to J$1. Take buses back and forth for J$0.80 between New Kingston (Halfway Tree) and downtown (Parade). Within these two areas, you should be able to walk most places you'll need to go.

SIGHTS

downtown: The Parade, where local militia once drilled, has been transformed into a magnificent park. On one side of the Parade is Kingston Parish Church. Reconstructed in 1909, the current building was modeled after the original which was destroyed in the 1907 earthquake. The Ward Theatre stands on a site which has been used continually for drama performances for centuries. Built in 1911, and open every year from 26 Dec. (Boxing Day) until April or May, it's home to the annual Pantomime, a national institution. Duke Street contains some noteworthy buildings, including the island's only Jewish Synagogue (The United Congregation of Israelites), St. Andrew Scots Kirk Church, and Gordon House, home of Jamaica's Parliament. Facing Gordon House is Headquarters House, one of the most historic buildings in Jamaica. Originally named Hibbert House after the man who built it, the name was changed after it became military headquarters in 1814 for the resident British military commander. It was constructed after Thomas Hibbert bet three other merchants in the 1750s to see who could build the finest and most elegant house. Of the four homes built, only Headquarters House remains standing. In 1872 it became the office of the Colonial Secretary and the meeting place for Jamaica's legislature. After the

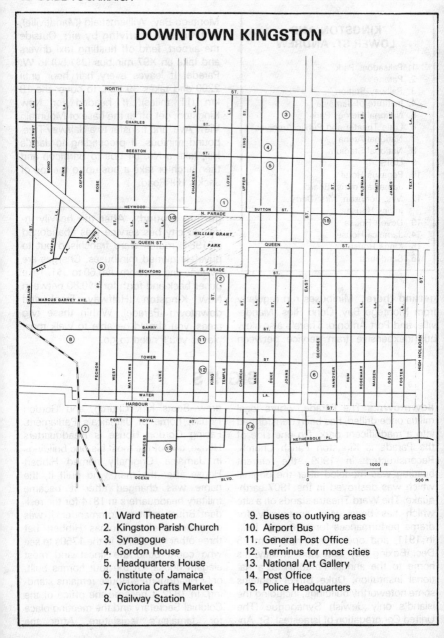

DOWNTOWN KINGSTON

1. Ward Theater
2. Kingston Parish Church
3. Synagogue
4. Gordon House
5. Headquarters House
6. Institute of Jamaica
7. Victoria Crafts Market
8. Railway Station

9. Buses to outlying areas
10. Airport Bus
11. General Post Office
12. Terminus for most cities
13. National Art Gallery
14. Post Office
15. Police Headquarters

legislature moved to Gordon House in 1960, Headquarters House remained vacant until the Jamaica National Trust Commission moved its headquarters here in 1983. Vale Royal, on Montrose Rd., is the prime minister's residence. The house, which has been in continuous use as a residence since the late 17th C., has a lookout tower on the roof which was used to keep track of the movement of ships in the harbor. National Heroes Park, along the way to Cross Roads, has modern monuments dedicated to national heroes George William Gordon and Paul Bogle, as well as the tombs of Marcus Garvey, Alexander Bustamante, and Norman Manley.

museums: The National Art Gallery, Kingston Mall, located in the Roy West Building at the corner of Ocean Blvd. and Orange St., has one of the most outstanding collections in the Caribbean (open Mon. to Sat., 1000-1700, J$1 suggested contribution). The ground floor is dominated by Christopher Gonzales' gigantic bronze of Bob Marley; the upstairs is divided into chronological periods beginning with early Intuitives like John Dunkley and David Miller. Also included is nearly everything Edna Manley ever sculpted, works by Carl Abrahams and Karl Parboosingh, stellar fantasies by Tina Matkovic and Colin Garland, and artwork by later Intuitives like Sidney McLaren. One entire room is packed with the products of the presiding genius of Jamaican art, Kapo (Mallica Reynolds). The Annual National Exhibition, featuring works by the island's best artists, is held here from Dec. through February. At its headquarters on East St., the Institute of Jamaica (Mon. to Fri., 0900-1700) has a small Natural History Museum; special exhibits are held on the floor above it.

The Coin and Note Museum is in the Bank of Jamaica building along the waterfront. Forces Museum, containing military memorabilia, is on Up Camp Road.

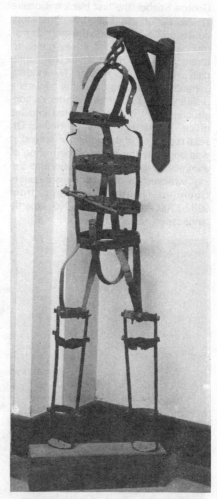

stocks: *This example of the severe punishment meted out to slaves comes from the Institute of Jamaica's collection.*

Devon House and vicinity: On Hope Rd. past Halfway Tree. Gleaming white and attractively landscaped, this stunning example of Georgian architecture has been restored by the National Trust. George Stiebel, the first black millionaire in the Caribbean, built this three-story house in 1881. Shops on the grounds surrounding the house sell pricey goods to foreigners and rich Jamaicans (open daily, 0900-1700). Farther N, modern Jamaica House was the prime minister's residence for a short period after its construction until it was converted into his office. Farther still is King's House. Official residence of the governor general, it was originally the home of the bishop of Jamaica. It was rebuilt two years after being wrecked in the 1907 earthquake. Open to visitors weekdays from 0900-1700, it is set amidst 200 expertly landscaped acres.

Hope Botanical Garden and Zoo: On 200 acres of land on the N side of Old Hope Rd., these gardens were laid out in 1881 after the government acquired the land from the Hope Estate. Originally an experimental garden, they were transformed into the Royal Botanical Gardens for the occasion of Queen Elizabeth's 1953 visit. In addition to the orchid house, there are Indonesian sago palms, a small zoo, a children's amusement park, and a stone aqueduct (open daily 0800-1800, J$0.50 admission).

University of the West Indies: Located along Mona Rd. in E. Kingston, this attractive campus has a unique history. Originally the site of the Mona Sugar Estate, there are ruins of mills, aqueducts, and a now silent water wheel. The original wooden buildings here were used as a center for Jewish refugees dur-

Devon House

ing WW II. The Chapel, located near the main entrance, was originally a sugar warehouse at Gales Valley Estate in Trelawny before it was dismantled stone by stone and reassembled here. Note that the original owner's name and date of construction can be seen along the top of the pediment just under the roof. The crests of the members of this international university are set inside the chapel.

recording studios: Must-see sites for reggae fans. Fortress-like Tuff Gong Studios (formerly Chris Blackwell's house and then Bob Marley's) is at 56 Oak Road. An Ethiopian flag flies outside above walls decorated with painted replicas of Marley album covers. Inside, there's a small record shop. Bunny Wailer's Solomonic Studio is at Ritriment Crescent, Cross Roads; Joe Gibb's studio is in Ritriment Road.

SHOPPING

markets: Victoria Market (closed Sun.) is the local handicraft market, which caters to visiting cruise ships and tourists. Coronation Market, a short walk from the Parade, provides a vivid, fascinating contrast with its down-to-earth, hustle-and-bustle atmosphere. Papine, a much smaller market located near the U.W.I. campus, has market days on Thurs. and Saturdays. A flea market takes place on Sun. at the Drive In Theater in New Kingston.

books and records: Kingston Bookshop Ltd. is at 70B King Street. Sangster's, the largest chain store, has branches at 33 King St., 97 Harbour St., 144 Old Hope Rd., and at 101 Water Lane. Times Store is at 8 King St., and Intellect Bookstore is at 20 Spanish Crescent. Books are also sold at the sales counter inside the Institute of Jamaica. Innumerable stores sell reggae albums. Try Randy's and Joe Gibb's on the Parade any of the chain of Music Fare shops, or the African Museum at 2 Chancery Lane, N. Parade. Many shops are on Orange St., including Bunny Wailer's Cash and Carry, Augustus Pablo's, Tuff Gong, and Prince Buster. Music City is on E. Queen St. and Aquarius is on Halfway Tree Road. High Times in Kingston Mall has an exceptionally good selection. Discounts for quantity available at Sonic Sounds, Ritriment Road.

art galleries: Great places to window shop. Upstairs Downstairs, Harbour St., features some of Jamaica's most renowned artists. Frame Center is at Tangerine Place off Halfway Tree Road. Bolivar Gallery, corner Halfway Tree and Grove roads, also contains a small bookshop. Mutual Life Gallery, corner Oxford and Old Hope roads, has assorted works by local artists. Olympia Art Center is at the end of Old Hope Rd. near Papine.

PRACTICALITIES

accommodations: New Kingston is the safest and most convenient area to base yourself. Retreat Guest House, 19 Seaview Ave., has rooms for J$20 pp (tel. 927-8853). Mrs. Johnson and Mrs. Derry, Nos. 2 and 7 Holburn Rd., have rooms available at negotiable rates. Mrs. Johnson's has more privacy, and her rates include breakfast. A longstanding favorite with Peace Corps volunteers, Green Gables Guest House, 6 Cargill Ave., New Kingston, has rooms for J$40 s and J$50 d (tel. 926-6711). A refundable key deposit of J$30 is charged. Sand-

hurst, 70 Sandhurst Crescent, charges from US$22 s and US$26 d (plus 10 percent service charge). Remember, higher-priced accommodations are subject to 10 percent service charge as well as US$8 and US$4 summer room tax. Indies Hotel, 5 Holburn Rd. (tel. 92-62989/62952), charges from US$16.50 s and US$39 d. The Kensington, 15-15 Kensington Crescent (tel. 92-92455), charges from US$25 s, US$35 d. Sutton Place Hotel, 11 Ruthven Rd. (tel. 92-62297), offers rooms at US$40 s and d. Medallion Hall Limited, 53 Hope Rd. (tel. 92-75721/75866),

KINGSTON ACCOMMODATIONS

HOTEL	ADDRESS	TEL.	HIGH SIN.	HIGH DBL.	HIGH TAX	LOW SIN.	LOW DBL.	LOW TAX	SERVICE
Indies Hotel	5 Holburn Rd.	926-0989 926-2952	17	29	8	19	32	4	5%
The Kensington	15-15½ Kensington Crescent	929-2455	25	35	8	25	35	4	
Mayfair Hotel	4 West Kings House Close (P.O. Box 163)	926-1610	30	35	8	30	35	4	10%
Medallion Hall Ltd.	53 Hope Rd.	927-5721 927-5866	35	40	8	35	40	4	10%
Pine Grove Guest House	Content, St. Andrew	922-3855	17	17	8	17	17	4	10%
Sandhurst	70 Sandhurst Crescent	927-8244 927-7239	20	22		20	22		10%
Sutton Place Hotel	11 Ruthven Rd.	926-2297	40	40	8	40	40	4	
Tropical Inn	19 Clieveden Ave.	927-9917 927-9918	45	55	10	45	55	6	

All prices are US$. High season: Dec. 15-April 30. Low season: May 1-Dec. 14. All rates listed are lowest. Higher rates may apply. Accommodation tax applied on a per day, per room basis.

charges from US$35 s. Downtown alternatives include the Green Lantern, 5 Ripon Rd. (Cross Roads area) and Duke's, corner Duke and Queen streets. One further alternative would be to stay or camp at Maya on Jack's Hill (see "Jack's Hill" under "Blue Mountains," and Chart for further accommodations.)

food: Many reasonably priced restaurants are located around Half Way Tree, Cross Roads, and downtown areas. Many moderately expensive restaurants (Indian, Middle Eastern cuisine) are located along Holburn Road. Lynn's Vegetarian at Tangerine Place off Half Way Tree Rd. serves soups, fish and vegetable dishes, and desserts. Meals start from J$7 (open daily 0830-2100). MacDonald's (a local imitation) is a fast-food joint across the road. Also try the Soup Kitchen nearby. For Indian food try Qualquanan on Hope Road or The Princess on the corner of Old Hope Road. Kensington Crescent serves authentic Chinese food. Rasta *ital* (vegetarian) cuisine at the Ethiopian, Old Hope Road. Also try Mimi's Ethopian Herbal on the same street. Morales, 46 Church St. (downtown), has fresh juices. Parkview Restaurant, on the Parade, has delicious Jamaican food. Try Try Me at Cross Roads. For midnight cravings go to Gino's, Spanish Court Plaza, Monty's, Old Hope Rd., or Hammond's, corner Duke and Queen Street—all three are open 24 hours. Road Runner chain stores have ice cream with local flavors. Good brown (Natural Bran) and corn (Black Lion Bakery) bread is baked in Kingston.

entertainment: Believe it or not there's no place in Kingston where you can go to hear reggae music every evening. Check posters to see what's on where. Bohemia Disco, Hagley Park Plaza (near Half Way Tree) has weekly talent shows every

This giant fabricated fowl on Trafalgar Rd. advertises the "best dressed chicken in town."

Wednesday evening from 2300 featuring 10 contestants with a backup band. Many well-known musicians got their start here. Skateland, also at Half Way Tree, is the most famous club in Kingston. Zinc Fence Theater, located off Holburn Rd., once rehearsal studio for the reggae band Third World, has occasional concerts. Tropic Night Club, a disco, is at 5 Dumphries Road. Joe's Phase "1," Holburn Rd., has go-go dancing and occasional talent shows. Intense late-night jazz sessions are held on Tues. and Thurs. evenings at the Peagasus Hotel. No cover and the music begins at 2100. Concerts are held at Randy Williams Center on Hope Rd., at the indoor National Arena, and at the outdoor National Stadium. Reggae superjam here every December. Movie theaters include the Odeon at Half Way Tree, Carib at Cross

Roads, and at the Drive In (which also has seats!) off Holburn Road. The Ward Theater, center of N. Parade, has yearly performances of the Christmas Pantomime, performances by the National Dance Theater, and presentations of local plays. The Little Theater, Tom Redcam Drive, stages performances by the National Theater Dance Company and the Jamaican Folk Singers. Hookers stalk Trafalgar Road.

services and information: The Jamaican Tourist Board (tel. 92-69280, 92-98070) is located in the New Kingston Office Complex, 77-83 Knutsford Blvd., next to the New Kingston Hotel in the heart of New Kingston (Mon. to Fri. 0830-1630). General information and pamphlets on Jamaica may be obtained from Jamaica Information Service, 58A Half Way Tree Road. Banks (only a small black market here) are centered in New Kingston. The General Post Office, which has a philatelic service, is on Temple Lane downtown (open Mon. to Thurs., 0900-1700, Fri., 0900-1600, Sat., 0900-1300). Other major post offices are at Half Way Tree, Cross Roads, corner Barbican and Hope roads, Three Mile, and on Winward Rd. near Mountain View Road. To make reservations for the cabins at Gourie and in the Blue Mountains, contact the Forestry Dept. at 173 Constant Springs Rd. (tel. 42-667, 42-612). The U.S. Embassy is at 2 Oxford Rd., while the British High Commission is on Trafalgar Road. The German Embassy is at 10 Waterloo Rd., and the French Embassy is located at 60 Knutsford Boulevard. Immigration is at 230 Spanish Town Road. Take a bus from Half Way Tree to Three Miles before changing to a Spanish Town bus (open Mon. to Fri., 0900-1500).

libraries: National Library of Jamaica, located next door to the Institute of Jamaica on East St., has books and newspapers on file. It contains the largest collection of W. Indies material of any library in the world (open Mon. to Thurs., 0900-1700, Fri., 0900-1600, Sat., 0900-1300). Kingston and St. Andrew Parish Library is at 2 Tom Redcam Drive. The Afro Caribbean Institute (Mon. to Fri., 0900-1200), 11 Worth St., has a small library. United States Information Service (USIS: Mon. to Fri., 0900-1600) is on the first floor, Mutual Life Bldg., corner Oxford and Old Hope roads. The British High Commission (Mon. to Fri., 0830-1630), Trafalgar Rd., has a reading room. The Australian High Commission (Mon. to Thurs., 0800-1700, Fri., 0800-1230) has plenty of books from over, down and under.

from Kingston: Bus service is available to just about any point on the island. With the exception of Spanish Town/Mandeville buses which leave from Half Way Tree, most start from the vicinity of the Parade downtown. Ask around. Trains leave for Spanish Town, Williamsfield (Mandeville), and Montego Bay from Kingston's railway station located at the W end of Barry Street. **by air:** Direct or connecting flights are available to virtually any N. American destination. Air Jamaica and ALM fly to Port-au-Prince with Air Jamaica continuing on to San Juan. No direct flights to Santo Domingo are available. BWI flies into Antigua, Barbados, and Trinidad. Excursion fares (17 days) range in price from US$252-326. Air Jamaica flies to Georgetown, Grand Cayman for US$150 RT while BA flies to Nassau, the Bahamas for US$218 (17-day excursion fare). Leaving every half hour until 2200 from the Parade, the X97 minibus (J$1.50) takes 30 min. to cover the 18 km (11 miles).

VICINITY OF KINGSTON

PORT HENDERSON

Situated across the bay from Port Royal. Can be reached by bus either from Spanish Town, or Kingston via Three Miles. Once a bustling and prosperous embarcation point for Spanish Town, today Port Henderson is reduced to a small village next to a shopping center. During the 18th C., while Spanish Town was still the island's capital, it was the chief point of arrival for visitors. It became a flourishing health and vacation resort during the 19th C. when its cold-water bathing pool was known as The Spa. As Spanish Town's fortunes waned so did those of Port Henderson. After The Spa disappeared in the 1951 hurricane, so did most of Port Henderson's income and population. Although it has been restored and preserved by the Jamaica National Trust Commission, it remains virtually unknown and unvisited — even by Jamaicans.

sights: The ruins of the Green Castle great house overlook the harbor, along with those of the smaller Bullock's Lodge just below. The House of the Two Sisters was used by vacationing families up until 1914. Fire has destroyed the restored Old Water Police Station, but the Longhouse remains intact. Used as an inn and lodging house until 1898, its name comes from its rectangular shape. The small, handsome building of dressed stone which once housed the public latrine now contains government offices.

Fort Clarence and Hellshire: Originally settled by Arawaks, this arid but spectacularly scenic area plays host to the island's last remaining iguanas and conies (Jamaica's only indigenous land mammal). Take a bus from Half Way Tree to Three Miles (J$0.60), then walk down to the RR tracks where there's a Rastafarian pottery workshop. Then take another bus to the R, get off at Fort Clarence roundabout (J$1.40) and walk

Hellshire Hills

to Fort Clarence Beach (open Mon. to Fri., 1000-1700; Sat. to Sun., 0900-1700, free admission). Beautiful location, and almost exclusively a Jamaican crowd. Vendors are prohibited so there're no hassles. Continue along the beach to the R to Half Moon Bay Fishing Authority. Many stands here sell fried fish and bammy, festival (delicious sweet fried bread), and drinking coconuts (J$1.20). Continue along to find a desolate cactus and coral headland area which stretches along the coast. Just you and the birds and the sea. Follow the main road farther down in the same direction to find many deserted white sand beaches with underground coves. Two Sisters Cave, in this area, has an Arawak-inscribed petroglyph of a human face. Be careful of currents while swimming.

PORT ROYAL

Once known as the "City of Gold" and the "Babylon of the West," Port Royal is now an unimpressive fishing village, a mere shadow of its former self. Only a few historical sites remain to tell the tale of what was "the wickedest city in the world" when Kingston, across the bay, was still only the site of a hog corral.

getting there: Easiest way is to take the ferry (J$0.70) from the No. 1 Pier near the Victoria Crafts Market. (Departs Mon. to Fri. at 0600, 0700, 1000, 1230, 1430, 1700, 1830; Sat. at 0600, 0630, 0800, 0830, 1000, 1030, 1230, 1315, 1400, 1430, 1630, 1700, 1830, 1900; Sun. at 1130, 1430, 1630, 1830.) Sit on the top deck, bask in the sun, and take in the view. Otherwise, take a bus from Kingston to the beginning of the Palisadoes (the 10-mile spit of land that contains Norman Manley Airport) and hitch.

history: Originally named Cayo de Carena (Careening Cay) by the Spaniards who discovered it, the English initially named it Cagway or The Point. Recognizing its strategic importance, the English built Fort Cromwell (later Fort Charles) within a year of their arrival. Eventually it was ringed by a network of six forts, stationing 2,500 men. Soon, a town sprang up to service the needs of the traders and buccaneers (a polite term for pirates). Encouraged by the government, the buccaneers used Port Royal as a base for their attacks upon Spanish ports as well as a place to dispose of their ill-gotten gains. As the buccaneers proliferated, so did the number of prostitutes and goldsmiths; the ratio of taverns and rum shops grew to one for every 10 residents. More than 2,000 buildings were jammed on this small cay, some erected on pilings driven into the sand. Rents soared to equal those of the poshest areas of London. A legend in his own time, Welsh adventurer Henry Morgan was the most colorful figure to emerge out of Port Royal. Within a few years, he carried out

Henry Morgan

five daring, highly successful raids. His sacking of Panama in 1671, coming as it did after the signing of a peace treaty between Britain and Spain, caused him, along with his patron the governor, to be brought back to London to stand trial. Although Gov. Modyford was imprisoned in order to appease the Spaniards, Morgan was knighted and returned in triumph as Lt. governor. Another legendary figure of the same era, Britain's greatest naval hero, Admiral Horatio Nelson, was twice stationed in Port Royal.

earthquake of 1692: To many it seemed like divine retribution when this "City of Sin" was hit by a devastating earthquake and tidal wave on 7 June 1692. The tidal wave, which followed the third shock, tossed one ship onto the roofs of houses in the center of town; more than 200 survivors clambered aboard seeking shelter. Warehouses, wharves, and taverns were swallowed up in a matter of seconds as huge fissures appeared in the earth. More than 2,000 died in the cataclysm. Although settlers had joined the town to the Palisadoes by filling in the marshy swamps, Port Royal again became an island. The 13 acres of land were rebuilt, only to be scorched by fire in 1703, ending Port Royal's days of affluence. It did, however, remain a thriving merchant community until it was finally eclipsed by Kingston, and it remained as the Royal Navy's principal base in the Caribbean until the Navy abandoned it in 1905.

sights: Dull gray, restored St. Peter's Church (1725) replaced Christ Church, which sank into the sea during the 1692 earthquake. As you enter the building, a lady in her energetic eighties will jump on you with a carefully rehearsed spiel and will immediately point out Louis Galdy's plaque up on the wall. Galdy, swallowed up during the 1692 cataclysm, was thrown back up into the sea and survived. His tomb is in the churchyard. Other plaques commemorate sailors who died from yellow fever. Despite what you may be told, the silver communion plate found here probably did not belong to Henry Morgan. Nearby, Fort Charles, one of the oldest and best preserved of the island's forts, now sits back a considerable distance from the sea. Climb up on the quarterdeck to see where Horatio Nelson paced back and forth in 1779 while waiting for a French attack that never came. A small Maritime Museum has a surprisingly attractive collection of submarine cables, model ships, and information about 18th and 19th C. canoe making (open daily, 1000-1300, 1400-1700). Turn R at the Fort entrance and go straight to reach Giddy House, once the Royal Artillery Store. The National Museum of Historical Archaeology, at one time the Naval Hospital, has detailed archaeological exhibits, including Arawak artifacts, Samurai and Bedouin swords, a machete from Nanny Town, and bone wig-curlers excavated in Port Royal (open Sat. to Thurs., 1000-1700; Fri., 1000-1600, J$0.50 admission). Powerful praying at the yellow frame house nearby on Sun. afternoons.

others: Port Royal is famous for its fried fish and bammy. Try Miss Gloria's Top and Bottom shops (two locations). Take a fishing boat out to Lime Cay (J$10 RT); boat will return for you in the afternoon. Beautiful snorkeling on this uninhabited island where Rhygin' the bandit, immortalized in the movie *The Harder They Come,* was gunned down by police. Negotiate to go out to other cays nearby. Gunboat Beach is along Palisadoes Rd. past the airport.

SPANISH TOWN

Not only is Spanish Town the most historically fascinating of all Jamaica's towns, but its forthright, down-to-earth atmosphere makes it a pleasure to visit as well.

getting there: Take any bus marked "Spanish Town" from Half Way Tree for the half-hour, 20-km (12 mile) J$1.20 ride. From the bus station, go down Oxford St. and turn R and follow Wellington down to the Square. Spanish Town may also be approached from Port Henderson, Mandeville, Ocho Rios, or Linstead.

history: After the Spanish officially abandoned their first settlement at Sevilla la Nueva on the N coast in 1534, they established their capital here, calling it Villa de la Vega (town on the plain). Spanish Town was sacked several times by the English before being captured permanently in 1655. Enraged to find the town empty of valuables, conquering English troops burned and wrecked

much of it. Later, Spanish Town became the administrative hub of the island. Not only did the governor reside here, but the House of Assembly and the Courts of Justice were built here as well. A rivalry developed between Spanish Town and that upstart mercantile community, Kingston. Under the influence of unscrupulous Kingston merchants, the governor forced a bill through the legislature in 1755 which moved the capital to Kingston. Since the king had not assented to the bill, it was eventually proclaimed illegal. The reprieve was not permanent—and the capital was moved to Kingston permanently in 1872. As the plantation economy of the 19th C. withered away, so did the grandeur of Spanish Town.

sights: Cathedral Church of St. James, on Red Church St., stands on the site of the Spanish Chapel of the Red Cross which was destroyed by Cromwell's army. The rebuilt structure, converted to the Anglican sect, was destroyed by the 1712 hurricane. Reconstructed in 1714, the present weathered red brick structure is the second oldest (after Fort Charles)

*Spanish Town
kids*

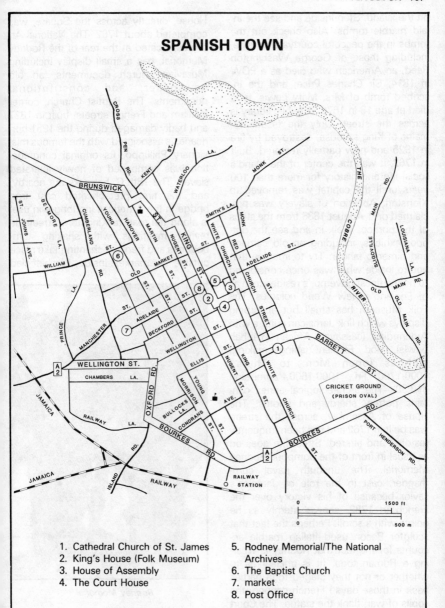

SPANISH TOWN

1. Cathedral Church of St. James
2. King's House (Folk Museum)
3. House of Assembly
4. The Court House
5. Rodney Memorial/The National Archives
6. The Baptist Church
7. market
8. Post Office

on the island. Step inside and see the inlaid marble tombs. Also check out the tombs in the peaceful courtyard outside, including those of George Washington Reed, an American who died as a POW in 1814; Sir Charles Price; and the inscribed tomb of Mrs. Mary Lewis, who died at age 18 in 1676. A public library is across the street. Only the facade remains of King's House, destroyed by fire in 1925 and now partially restored. Built in 1762, it was the center of the island's social life and history for more than 100 years until the capital was removed to Kingston. Abolition of slavery was proclaimed on 1 August 1838 from the steps of the portico. Walk in and see the outdoor exhibits, including an old carriage and pimento fanner. Try to imagine that you're inside what was once considered to be the finest governor's residence in all of England's New World colonies. The Folk Museum has small but absorbing displays which link Jamaican culture with Amerindian (cassava), African (Yabbah bowls), and English (shingle-making) cultures (open Mon. to Thurs., 1000-1700; Fri., 1000-1600, admission J$0.30). The archaeological annex contains pottery shards and photos. The House of Assembly, across the street, was built in 1762 and has been frequently restored and altered. Street life goes on as usual in front of the pompous Rodney Memorial. The uncouth naval commander, cast in the role of Jamaica's savior because of his victory over the French in 1782, scowls sternly as he points with a scroll. Perhaps the fact that sculptor Bacon used Italian marble accounts for the fact that Rodney is wearing a Roman toga. (It is unclear as to whether or not they staged toga parties back in those days.) French cannon, the spoils of war, flank the statue. The Court

House, directly across the Square, was completed about 1762. The National Archives, located at the rear of the Rodney Memorial, has a small display including Moravian church documents, an old newspaper, and constitutional documents. The Baptist Church, corner William and French streets, built in 1827 and badly damaged during the 1951 hurricane, is associated with the famous missionary Phillippo. Its original congregation was composed of newly liberated slaves. The 18th C. barracks are nearby, and the first prefabricated cast iron bridge in the Americas (no longer in use) is along the road to Kingston. Streetside revival meetings with shaking tambourines and frenzied chanting take place outside the market. Inside, kerchief-clad

Rodney Memorial

Third oldest Anglican church on the island, St. Peter's Church, in Alley, was originally built in 1671 and nearly totally rebuilt after the 1692 earthquake.

ladies sell piles of chicken legs, bundles of Kallaloo, and TDK T-shirts. A fish and bammy lady offers the genuine article behind the Rodney statue.

vicinity of Spanish Town: On the way to Kingston are the Cayamanas race track and the Arawak Indian Museum at White Marl. The latter has both indoor and outdoor displays of Indian remains and artifacts (open Mon. to Thurs., 1000-1700; Fri., 1000-1600; admission J$0.30). To the N in the hills, Sligoville was once the summer home of the governor; it was established by the Baptist Rev. J.M. Phillippo. Purchasing the land in 1835, the town he started became the first post-emancipation free village in the W. Indies. Linstead is a celebrated market town. Guanaboa Vale, 15 km (nine miles) NW of Spanish Town, has a church with interesting tombstones. A famous colonial mutiny occurred here in 1660. Mountain River Cave, near the town, contains Arawak petroglyphs of hunters, birds, and turtles. Farther on to the N, Lluidus Vale has a 300-year-old sugar plantation. At Old Harbour Bay W of Spanish Town, Columbus sighted manatees for the first time, initially mistaking them for mermaids (Columbus was either extremely horny or extremely nearsighted!). Little Goat I. offshore was a U.S. Naval Base from 1942-49. Colbeck Castle, 2.4 km NW of Old Harbour, is a mysterious building. Practically nothing is known of the origin of what was once the largest building on the island save that it was built by the unpopular Col. John Colbeck in the 17th or 18th centuries. May

Pen, an unappealing town of 40,000, is the capital of Clarendon Parish. To the S is Vere, formerly (owing to its production of indigo dye) one of the most prosperous districts in Jamaica. Once a separate parish, its capital was Alley, whose church, St. Peter's (1715), is noted for its bell and church organ. The entire courtyard is very English in appearance. On the W bank of the Milk River to the SW of May Pen lies Milk River Bath, which has a radioactivity level much higher than that of any other mineral spa in the world. Reach here by taking transport from Four Paths outside May Pen. Stay at the small hotel. Farquahr Beach is three km (almost two miles) to the south. A track N of Milk River heads W along the coast to Alligator Pond. Porus, in the main road to Mandeville from May Pen, is well-known for its citrus fruits.

THE BLUE MOUNTAINS

Named for the haze that glazes their peaks the better part of each day, the Blue Mountains are undoubtedly the most unusual travel destination in Jamaica. Few people envision Jamaica as having cool woodlands, engulfed at times in a sea of heavy mist, but that is exactly what the Blue Mtns. have to offer. Forming the interior of Portland, St. Thomas, and St. Andrew, their consistently cool climate averages around 15 degrees C (65 F). Heaved up from the floor of the Caribbean 25 million years ago, they are growing at a rate of one foot per thousand years. Dominating the Eastern Highlands, the Grand Ridge of the Blue Mountains contains many prominent peaks, all more than 1,640 m (5,000 ft.) and many are more than 1,968 m (6,000 ft.). From E to W, the peaks are

Sugar Loaf, John Crow, and Silver Hill. Rounded, conical Blue Mountain Peak, highest on the island, is 2,256 m (7,402 feet). Once heavily timbered, the southern slopes of the Grand Ridge are being deforested at an alarming rate. The presence of rangers patrolling the terrain has not deterred local farmers who continue to clear land illegally in order to plant ganja and other crops. This is not the case with the side facing Portland, however, where torrential rainfall has left the rugged terrain virtually unexploited. Far to the E, the mountains collide with the much lower (3,000 ft.) John Crow Mountains. The Port Royal Mountains, a subsidiary range which affords Kingston its dramatic backdrop, run to the southeast.

getting there and around: A number of roads run around and through the mountains. A3, the main route to Annotto Bay, passes through Castleton, skirting the E edge. From Kingston a road runs up to the suburb of Jack's Hill and on to Hollywell and other destinations. Another road on the E side of Kingston heads up to The Cooperage, where it splits to the E for Mavis Bank and Blue Mtn. Peak. The W half of the fork leads on to Irish Town, Redlight, Newcastle, and Hardwar Gap before connecting with the road for Buff Bay. These main routes are supplemented by innumerable footpaths and shortcuts. Virtually no transport heads up this way, so unless you have your own vehicle, count on walking a great deal.

practicalities: Places to stay and camp in this area are listed in the text under specific localities. Cabins at Hollywell or Clydesdale may be rented from the Forestry Department, 173 Constant Spring Rd., Kingston (tel. 42-667, 42-668). Reservations should be made one month in advance if planning to arrive on a weekend. Although pots and pans are provided, it's best to bring your own as they are occasionally stolen. For Whitfield Hall Hostel reservations, phone John Algrove at 70986 or U.D.C. at 28310, 28314. Remember to bring your own food, as restaurants and food stores, when available at all, are few and far between.

JACK'S HILL

No longer city but not yet country, this outlying suburb is a great place to make the transition from urban to rural life. In this small village, strung out along the side of the road, there's little save a post office, bar and store, a pay phone that is perpetually out of order, an outdoor auto repair shop, and the ubiquitous police station with the officers lazing about. There are great views of Kingston however, and magnificent sunsets may be seen from the top of the water tower. Owing to the irregular transportation, it's hardly a convenient place to stay if interested in checking out Kingston's nightlife, though it's a perfect place of departure for exploring the Blue Mountains. To get here take bus or minivan No. 12 (J$1) or hitch up along steep Jack's Hill Rd. from the end of Kingston's Barbicon Road. A trail along Peter's Rock Rd. leads to Cambridge and then Hollywell and Hardwar Gap. Peter Bentley, head of the Jamaican Hiking and Camping Association, offers accommodation and guides (US$10 per day) for exploring the area. He also offers comprehensive tours and charges US$6 per night for accommodation and US$4 pp per night for camping. His home and base (tel. 927-0357), Maya, is at the end of Jack's Hill Rd. past Vinnie's Auto Shop. Take good care to secure your gear if staying here.

CLYDESDALE AND CINCHONA

Clydesdale: Only an inoperative water wheel plus drying and roasting pits serve as a reminder that this seedling nursery was once a coffee plantation. A cabin rented out by the Forestry Dept. has the sayings of Rastafarian A.A. Peters featured on the walls inside. The kitchen and living room areas are attractively furnished. Charges are J$20 weeknights or J$90 for five nights and J$50 for Sat. and Sunday. Bring all of your food and cooking supplies as none are available. Bathe in the river pool nearby. Trails lead to Morces and St. Helens Gaps.

Cinchona Botanic Gardens: Spec-

VICINITY OF
BLUE MOUNTAIN PEAK

tacularly set along a 1,527-m (5,000-ft.) ridge, Cinchona Botanic Gardens was named after the tree from whose bark quinine is obtained. Established as a cinchona and Assam tea plantation in 1868, it shrank over the years, as profits dwindled, to the small flower and vegetable garden which remains. The numerous trees surrounding the great house are both indigenous and imported. Note the Blue Mtn. yacca with its small, dagger-shaped leaves. See workers picking coffee berries between Sept. and Feb. at the Silver Hill coffee factory (open daily 0600-1800).

getting there and vicinity: Take a No. 61 bus from Papine to Kingston up the steep, winding road to Irish Town via The Cooperage. Nothing remains of Jamaica's first botanical garden, established here in 1770. Follow the road along to Guava Ridge and try some free samples at "World's End," a distillery run by Scottish immigrant Ian Sangster. Continue on to Valda and then Content Gap where the L path from the water tower leads to Charlottenburg House, an old great house.

BLUE MOUNTAIN PEAK

The highlight of any trip in the Blue Mtns. should be climbing up Blue Mountain Peak. It's best to overnight at Whitfield Hall before attempting the strenuous three-hour climb. Most hikers rise in the dead of night (0200-0300) to begin the ascent in order to arrive at the top in time to view the resplendent sunrise. On a clear morning it's possible to see as far as Cuba. The forest along the way is composed of short, gnarled colorado trees, their branches laden with mosses, epiphytes, and ferns. At their bases look for enchanting dwarf orchids.

practicalities: Take a minibus from Papine to Mavis Bank. Then follow the 10-km bridle path from Mavis Bank to Whitfield Hall. Another way is to proceed from Clydesdale to Cinchona to Whitfield Hall. Whitfield Hall Hostel, near the village of Penlye Castle, has dorm beds (including a crib) for J$10. If you stay in your own tent, it's J$5 pp. Have a look

hiking in the Blue Mountains

Valley. Established in 1814 as a hill station for British troops at a time when, owing to the prevalance of disease, a sojourn on the coast was regarded as a certain death sentence, this former coffee plantation was gradually built up into the present day red-roofed buildings. The bar and Sergeant's Mess are available for use by visitors.

Hollywell: Situated a mile above Newcastle at 990 m (3,250 ft.) and covering an extensive 300 acres (120 ha), this forest reserve includes picnic tables and miles of hiking trails. An excellent place to stay for a few days and take day hikes, three cabins are for rent here. Cabin No. 1 has two bedrooms and rents for J$20 weeknights or J$90 Sun. to Thurs. or for J$50 for Fri. and Sat.; the other three cabins are equipped with twin beds, and rent for J$15 weeknights or J$60 for Sun. to Thurs., J$40 for Fri. and Sat. nights. Campers pay J$5 per night, but they must *also* be renting a cabin. All reservations must be made and prepaid at the Forestry Department in Kingston.

over the marvelous collection of antique books on the shelves of this simply but attractively furnished home, which was once the great house of a coffee plantation. Meals are served here upon request. Bring all food, cooking utensils, flashlight, sweater, and rain parka.

NEWCASTLE AND HOLLYWELL

Newcastle: Take the main road from Kingston past Irish Town to get to this Jamaica Defence Force Camp set high in the hills overlooking the Mamee River

Castleton: The main road from Kingston to Annotto Bay passes through these gardens. Established in 1859, time and the continual flooding of the Wag Water River have reduced its splendor. Once the richest botanical garden in the entire Caribbean, it's still well worth a visit. Strychnos trees, from which strychnine is obtained, stand in the upper section of the garden. Mahogany and Burmese teak may be seen in the lower section (open 0700-1800 daily).

SOUTH AND WEST JAMAICA

MANDEVILLE

A fairly large, extremely scattered town, this is the capital of Manchester Parish. Although Mandeville has long been compared to an English country town, its Continental character is swiftly fading as it becomes a carbon copy of American suburbia with shopping centers and Kentucky Fried Chicken. The area surrounding the Manchester Club, which has the island's oldest golf course, still retains a distinctly English feeling. Although at the time of its establishment in 1814 it was a playground for landed European gentry, expatriates today are predominantly Americans working in the bauxite industry, which has brought relative prosperity to this area. Mandeville is definitely a place to beat the heat; the temperature here ranges from the 60s during the winter to the 70s during the summer. The area's most famous product is the *ortanique*. Developed here about 1920 by

C.P. Jackson, the name for this seedless, extremely juicy fruit was coined by combining the words "orange, tangerine and unique."

getting there and around: Most easily reached by bus or minibus from Kingston (via Spanish Town) or from Black River. Or take a train to Williamsfield from Montego Bay or Kingston, then a minibus or shared taxi on to Mandeville. There's no local bus system so you'll either have to walk or bargain with the drivers of shared taxis.

SIGHTS

All of the major streets slope up to Mandeville Square where the park, market, courthouse and rectory are located. Surrounded by a sea of modernity, the anachronistic courthouse was built with limestone blocks cut by slaves. Completed around 1820, the design underwent many modifications before it was finished. Standing to the L of the courthouse, what was once Mandeville's rectory is still the oldest house in town. Rented out as a tavern, it was later used as a guest house before being converted to a private residence. Also on the central green, Manchester Parish Church opened its doors in 1820. Mandeville Hotel, an old landmark on Hotel St., was originally a barracks for English troops before being converted to a hotel during the 1890s. It has long been a place of retirement for many expatriate British. Marshall's Pen is an 18th-C. great house set in the middle of a 300-acre cattle farm. Manchester Green Farm and Stables, located 2.5 km

S of town atop Huntingdon Summit, appears from the distance to be a gigantic, futuristic green Chinese pagoda—almost appearing as if a spacecraft full of Oriental aliens had landed on top of the hill. Horses and cows graze on the green, fenced-in pastures along the way up to this octagonal mansion owned by Mandeville's mayor and former sno-cone salesman Cecil Charleton. Outside, birdcages containing cockatoos and other tropical exotics hang near a fountain built in the shape of a map of Jamaica and a walkway representing the Jamaican flag. An outdoor swimming pool flows under the walls into the living room where it transforms into a small pond. Get permission to view the estate; tel. 962-2247/2493. Tours of Alcan's Kirkvine Works, NE of Mandeville, can be arranged by

the rolling hills of Clarendon Parish NE of Mandeville

phone. From the top of Shooter's Hill near the plant, a splendid panorama unfolds with Blue Mountain Peak clearly visible to the east.

PRACTICALITIES

accommodations: Villa House, slightly sleazy and next to Club Harmony, charges J$25 per room. Lor's Residential Inn, out of town near the bypass, is the same price. Also out of town is Mike Town Guest House (take a Green Hill taxi) and Roden Guest House, 6 Wesley Avenue. Arthur Sutton at Marshall's Pen (tel. 962-2260) has rooms available for US$5 pp and camping at US$3 pp. Mandeville Hotel, 40 Hotel Square (tel. 962-2138), charges from US$16 s and US$20 d (subject to US$8 winter tax and US$4 room tax).

food: At Capri Restaurant and Coffeeshop, next to Odeon Theater, a pleasing mixture of expatriates and locals hang out. Try the wonderful *ital* (vegetarian) special. Crazy Jim's has a well-rounded selection of fast food; La Favourita is good for breakfast with an egg salad sandwich and coffee for J$2.70. Mrs. Meyers' Unique Restaurant has meals for J$7. GG's and Hammond's on Manchester Rd. also have good food. Trevor's Snack and Restaurant is on S. Racecourse Road. For baked goods, Lynn's Bakery is on Ward Avenue. Marzouca's Deli, in Mandeville Plaza, has pickled, sinful-tasting Satan's Sauce and Pepperwind Pepper Jelly, used for seasoning meat. Also available are *dulce* (guava cheese) and guava liqueur. If you'd like a colorful environment, Spotlight Restaurant is set inside a wonderfully painted bus.

entertainment: Capri tends to be the liveliest place in town, with a live band on Fri. evenings. Also try the Tudor Club on Ward Ave., Green Lantern, and Ken's Cool Shade Bar. Discos include Planet Disco and In Time on Manchester Road. Performances are occasionally given at Cecil Charlton Hall in Manchester Parish Library.

shopping: Mandeville's extremely colorful market is set off to one side of Mandeville Square. Housed in a yellow building, squatting higglers flow out the doors onto the sloping driveway along the entrance where they sell yams, green peppers, cassava, white turnips, oranges, green bananas, ginger, beans and sugarcane. Also outside there's usually a revivalist group present with a lady, wearing a white turban, reading from the Bible and holding a white flag. Inside, the meat market has individually apportioned stalls with cow and goat heads for sale. Fishes of all sizes, shapes and colors are sold from tin washing pans.

services and information: The local branch of Jamaica Information Service is across from NCB on Mandeville Plaza (open Mon. to Thurs., 0830-1700; 0830-1600 on Friday). The Baha'i Centre on Caledonia Rd. has meetings Sun. afternoons at 1530.

from Mandeville: Buses and minibuses leave regularly for Black River and Montego Bay. For Treasure Beach take a minibus as far as Santa Cruz and then change. If taking the train to Montego Bay or Kingston, call up the train station in Williamsfield (tel. 962-4213).

*Alcan's
Kirkvine
works*

VICINITY OF MANDEVILLE

The whole area surrounding Mandeville has much to offer. Since it's unfrequented by tourists or visitors, you're pretty far off the beaten track, so finding transport may be difficult.

to the north: The bauxite mining operation of Alcan's Kirkvine Works dominates the valley to the NE of Mandeville. The Pickapepper factory, home of Jamaica's famous version of Worcestershire Sauce, is at the crossroads of Rtes. B4, 5, and 6. Mile Gully has an attractive 19th C. church, while Grove Place has the largest livestock breeding research station on the island. Situated at 846-m (2,750-ft.) elevation about three km N of Christiana is Gourie Recreation Center (enter near Coleyville Banana Plant). With an average mean temperature of 68 degrees F, Gourie is an attractive place to stay for relief from the heat. In addition to numerous hiking trails, there's also the Gourie Cave, source of the Black River. Two cabins here furnished ''country style'' have two beds, gas stove and utensils. Bring your own sleeping bags or blankets and sheets as well as food. In order to stay here, reservations (with advance payment) must be obtained from the Forest Dept., 173 Constant Spring Rd., Kingston (tel. 42-667/42-612). Charges are J$40 to rent a cabin for Fri. and Sat. nights, and J$60 for Sun. through Thurs. nights (or J$15 per night excluding Fri. and Saturday).

to the south: Marlborough House, at Spur Tree, built in 1795, is a fine example of a late 18th C. Palladium great house. Ask permission to visit. Get a fantastic view from the Alcan parking lot at the top of Spur Tree Hill. Alligator Pond, a quiet fishing village, has an early morning fish market. Locals rent out cottages. Unless you're driving a jeep, plan to walk the 30 km (18 miles) through aptly named Gut River to Milk River. Off to one side of the road is God's Veil, a 50-m (160-ft.)-deep limestone sinkhole with sparkling turquoise water. Named by a man who claimed to have been cured of a terminal illness by bathing here. You might see manatees at Cano Valley.

THE SOUTHWEST COAST

TREASURE BEACH

This gem of a beach area is located in one of Jamaica's remotest regions. Almost completely isolated with no phones or newspapers and little rainfall, four small bays (Great, Calabash, Frenchman's, and Billy's) are connected by road with the small town of Treasure Beach. Yellow and red fishing boats line the brown sand beach at Calabash Bay. Frenchman's Bay has the best beach, though it's crowded Sundays. Good hiking in this area—especially along the bluff from Great Bay. Locals, some of whom are said to be the descendants of shipwrecked Scottish seamen, are among the friendliest in all Jamaica. Most famous of them is Chrissie James, a basketmaker who won the Jamaica 21 competition, held in celebration of the island's independence.

getting there: From Mandeville take a minibus to Santa Cruz, then change to a vehicle for Pedro Cross or Treasure Beach. Or approach from Mountainside or the smaller of the two Lacovias.

Transportation is extremely irregular, so count on long waits both ways.

practicalities: A great range and variety of guest houses (yes, houses!) rent from J$40 and up. One that sleeps 16 costs J$80 per night. Prices are lowest on weekdays. Locals may put you up or have rooms for rent—ask around. Great Bay Coop is the best-stocked shop in the area. Weekly markets are held in Calabash and Great Bays on Fridays. Buy fresh fish and lobster directly from fishermen; the best time is from 1200-1300 Mon. and Friday.

BLACK RIVER

The curving A2 highway runs right through this pretty town set along the coast, dividing the sea from the deteriorating but colorful gingerbread houses. This sleepy fishing village, once a major logging center, explodes with color and activity on Fri. and Sat. when the covered market is held. Alligators still lurk upriver. For safer swimming, continue on to Belmont and Bluefields beaches. Stay at Waterloo Guest House, an attractive two-story blue-and-green house, J$25 s, J$30 d. Large rooms are equipped with bath and toilet, with a moderately priced restaurant downstairs. This was the first house in Jamaica to have had electricity put in. Other hotels include the Pontio and Bridgehouse. Try the peppered shrimp at Middlequarters, 13 km (eight miles) south. The Holland Estate and sugar factory is near the junction of A2 and the oddly named Y.S. River. Find the overrated "Bamboo

Avenue," a stretch of bamboo-shaded road acclaimed as a tourist attraction on the way to Lacovia.

SAVANNA-LA-MAR

The name of this undistinguished sugar port means "plain by the sea." Few towns in the world have been devastated more frequently by hurricanes than Sav-La-Mar. The 1748 hurricane left ships beached, the 1780 hurricane completely destroyed the town, and the one in 1912 cast the schooner *Laconia* into the middle of the main street. Not much to see here except the fort which has long served as an improvised swimming pool. In 1755 a visiting admiral declared it to be the very worst fort on the island. From Bluefields

to the S, Henry Morgan sailed to sack Panama in 1670. A small sand beach skirts the white bay here. At Pelican Hole, near the bridge over the Bluefields River, two enormous birches and a fig tree shelter pelicans, frigate birds and boobies. Some crumbling walls still stand at Oristan where Spaniards founded the short-lived settlement of Oristan in 1509. Obtain permission to view the remains by writing to Bluefields Estate, Westmoreland Parish. Rumored to have been built to house Napoleon, the ruined 19th-C. castle on the grounds of Auchindown Farm was built by one Archibald Campbell. Its two towers are—rather absurdly—connected underground. See the early morning fish market at Whitehouse where dugout canoes are still constructed.

THE WESTERN INTERIOR

SEAFORD TOWN

Near the village of Rat Trap stands what is probably Jamaica's most unusual village—the only one consisting almost entirely of fair-skinned, blue-eyed farmers. First settled by a band of 570 from Bremen, Germany, in 1835, another thousand or so came to settle during the succeeding eight years. Created a baron in 1826, Lord Seaford granted 500 acres of his Westmoreland estate in response to a government plea for land grants to encourage European immigration to replace slave labor. Although each immigrant was granted from three to 23 acres, the land was mountainous and lacked irrigation water—basically unarable. Free rations were provided by the Jamaican government for the first 18

months, but the settlers had to walk 19 km to Chester Castle to pick them up. Population plummeted under the effects of malnutrition and yellow fever, but the hardy Germans stayed on. In recent years the population has decreased because of emigration. Inbreeding has reduced the number of family names to only 15, with Kameke being the most prominent. Although there has been interbreeding with blacks, most of these marriages were with younger sons and daughters of the community who, lacking the right to inherit land, chose to settle outside. Although a few houses of distinctive architectural style and some customs remain, no living soul here can speak a word of German. A museum near the Sacred Heart Catholic Church contains a list of family names and other memorabilia.

COCKPIT COUNTRY

formation: Viewed from the air, this potholed limestone plateau resembles nothing so much as a series of meshed cardboard egg containers covered with a green carpet of vegetation. Stretching over a 500-sq-mile area, it covers the southern half of Trelawny Parish and extends over to the E edge of St. James and then down to the N tip of St. Elizabeth. The enormous, craggy limestone pits that give the region its name are a result of a unique geological process called karstification. Just five million years ago the terrain was flat. Over a million-year period, heavy rains seeped through the primary structural lines and joints of the porous limestone terrain, carving huge caves, deep sinkholes, and long underground passages. Now lush, verdant vegetation masks the treacherous pits. Inaccessible to all but the hardiest adventurer, they remain virtually unexplored even today.

the Maroons: The only group of people to ever attempt to tame the pits did so out of sheer necessity. These people were the Maroons. After the British invaded Jamaica in 1655, it took five years to crush the last armed Spanish resistance. During this period, African slaves, left to their own resources, took to the inaccessible areas of the Cockpit country and the Blue Mountains, grouping together for self-defense. Around 1662 they became known as the Maroons. No one is certain of the name's derivation, but it's thought to have come from the French *marron*, which means "runaway slave." Another possibility is that it might be a corruption of the Spanish *cimarran*, meaning "wild or untamed." The Maroons were able to exist in the harsh environment of the cockpits because some of the pit bottoms were flat and tillable. Many are as large as baseball fields; the site of Petty River Bottom, a former Maroon camp, measures seven acres. Maroon settlements in the Blue Mountains and in the cockpits became havens for runaway slaves. Soon, a guerrilla war began which stretched over 80 years. In 1663 the British attempted to settle with the implacable Maroons, but an envoy sent to sue for peace was cut to pieces instead. From 1690 to 1720, Maroons raided plantations for livestock and goods. The British responded by organizing bands of armed slaves and im-

Maroon warrior

porting Indians from Cuba to go after the Maroons. The Maroons were split into two groups: the Leeward Maroons led by Kojo (or Kudjoe), and the Windward Maroons in Portland Parish, led by Quao, Kofi, and the legendary Nanny (see "Nannytown" under "Vicinity of Port Antonio").

Maroon autonomy: Conceding defeat at last in 1738, the British signed a peace treaty with Kojo on 1 March 1739. Legal autonomy (which theoretically stands to this day) was granted along with ownership of 2,500 acres to be used for farming and hunting. The Windward Maroons signed an agreement shortly thereafter. The role of the Maroons changed dramatically from that of protectors of runaway slaves to slave hunters. Called in to suppress rebellions, Maroons killed the rebel leader Tacky Blue in 1760. But the peace did not last forever. In 1759, in clear violation of a treaty provision stating that only Maroons could administer justice to Maroons, two Trelawny Maroons were whipped after being caught red-handed stealing a pig in Montego Bay. This incident, coupled with a desire for more land, incited the community to war again. The 600 Trelawnys were met by a force of 1,500 British troops equipped with Cuban bloodhounds; these terrifying dogs caused the Maroons to sue for peace. Agreeing to the Maroon's stipulation that they were not to be executed or transported, they were instructed by the government to surrender within a few days. After the last of them had straggled in on 21 March, the governor declared that treaty conditions had been violated and shipped them off to Halifax, Nova Scotia. After four harsh winters, they were sent to Sierra Leone on the W. coast of Africa. Although Trelawny Town has disappeared, the old Maroon Town Barracks remain at Flagstaff near Maroon Town. Fascinating to visit. Nowadays, there's little to differentiate the Maroon from any other Jamaican. Rasta influence and television have taken their toll, and a police station now stands in the chief Leeward Maroon settlement of Accompong.

Accompong: A beaten and pitted road leads up to this primitive mountain village, named after Maroon leader Kojo's brother. Most of the people here are descendants of the Akan-speaking peoples of W. Africa. A schoolteacher and preacher, Col. Harris Cawley is the leader of these Maroons, who celebrate Kojo's birthday here every 6 January. Complex drumming commences at daybreak, and the villagers make a pilgrimage to Accompong's grave and the *ceiba* tree where the treaty with the British was signed. The day's celebration ends with a reggae dance party in the evening.

Elderslie: Camp here for US$3 pp per night on a lush five-acre site next to the mouth of a large cave from which runs a clear stream. Ask Mrs. Maize at the general store in town if you wish to stay with a family.

THE WEST COAST

NEGRIL

On the SW tip of Westmoreland Parish and protected by an offshore reef, this 11-km stretch of sand is one of the finest beaches in the Caribbean. Wade out to your waist in crystal-clear water the color of emeralds; see right down to the white sand bottom. Once a traveler's paradise, Negril now qualifies as an up-and-coming Miami Beach, well on the way to holding the dubious distinction of being the worst tourist trap on the island. It has become a ghetto for middle- and upper-class North Americans and Europeans, imitation Rastas, and home to at least half of the hawkers of tourist services (the other half base themselves at MoBay and Ocho Rios). Just walk along the beach for a moment and they're on you like flies: "Anything to drink? Banana bread? Tie your hair into braids? Want to see a real Jamaican pussy, man?" Sundays are the worst because the kids are all out of school. Avoid hassles by walking in or along the water, wearing earplugs, or turning your Walkman up full blast. Another option might be to lie on the beach and lay out one beer, a piece of banana bread, some fruit, and a ganja spliff. Then you *might* be left alone. Another alternative is to come during the dry season, when higglers disappear like mosquitoes. Remember, however, this is how they make their daily *ackee,* and if you don't mind being in the center of a 11-km outdoor market, Negril is a great place!

history: Originally named Negrillo by the Spanish. In 1702 Admiral Benbow assembled his squadron for a voyage which ended with his defeat by the French. Captain Barnet captured pirate Calico Jack—so named because of his passion for calico underwear—along with his female crew members here in 1702. In 1814, the British flotilla left from here for New Orleans. Negril was redeveloped at

Negril beach

a cost of US$4.5 million in 1973 when a new highway and drainage canals were constructed. Around the same time, arriving hippies founded the site of Ganjaland on a forested track near the airport. Turning capitalist in the latter half of the '70s, they were responsible for bringing development to Negril.

getting there: Easily approached by minibus or bus from MoBay, Lucea, or Sav-La-Mar. In fact, owing to the persistence of touts who pack the minibuses, you may end up going there whether you intend to or not.

accommodations: Least expensive during the off season. If you don't have much gear, camping along the beach is the cheapest and best alternative. Sammy's charges J$7 for camping; J$5 at both Roots Bamboo and God's Love. Roots Bamboo rents tents for J$5 per night plus J$7 pp, and cabins for J$20.

Negril sunsets are famous for their beauty.

God's Love charges J$10 pp per night—cooking permitted; ask for Donovan. At Sammy's, rooms are J$25 s or d; up to four can share. More deluxe is Arthur's Golden Sunset where rooms are J$60 d. Bar-B-Barn's chalets hold up to four or more persons. Twin beds are upstairs, kitchenette, hot and cold running water, daybed downstairs; US$70 per day. At Red Ground, Aunt Pet Barrett Guest House has rooms for J$33. Many others are available in the same area. Bargain firmly. Many hotels line the road to the West End where Ric's Cafe is famous for its view at sunset. Negril Beach Villas, set up on a hill with tropical gardens and a swimming pool, rents for J$70 per unit per night.

food: Pricey like everything else. Beers alone are J$3 along the beach—twice the regular price. Always ask before you eat; otherwise, the sky's the limit. Corn soup is served on the bridge for J$1 per cup. Try the conch chowder at the wharf club and the jerk chicken at De Buss on the beach. Magic mushroom tea is J$4 per cup at Miss Cool along the beach. Mama Bee's, inside the straw market, has fresh fish dinners for J$8. Miss Brown's is a famous restaurant in a shack adjacent to the supermarket. She's famous for her mushroom tea.

entertainment: People tend to go to bed early. At the Rocky Edge, go-go dancers contort and twist their buns in a way that brings a sparkle to the eyes of Jamaican men. Soon Come Disco is near the shopping place, and there's hedonistic dancing at Hedonism II.

services and information: Plenty of people to change money with along the beach (at a slightly lower rate than

Fort Charlotte

MoBay's black market), but watch out for rip-off artists. Peter Bentley's Jamaica Camping and Hiking Association has its headquarters at Golden Sunset along Negril Beach (tel. 957-4241). It may be worth the trip to Negril just to meet Peter, one of the island's most ardent naturalists. Book reservations here for tours of the Blue Mtns. (US$40) and for accommodations island-wide.

from Negril: Minibuses leave regularly for Lucea (J$3.50), MoBay (J$6), Sav-La-Mar, Mandeville, etc.

LUCEA

Once a busy sugar port, it's still one of the best harbors on the N side of the island. An attractive town, it's the capital of Hanover Parish, smallest parish on the island and noted for "Lucea yam." Note the German helmet on the clock in the courthouse: it was sent by mistake. Like most such island tower clocks, this one is out of order.

sights: A short walk from town is Fort Charlotte. This classically designed 18th C. fort, named after George III's queen, stands on a peninsula overlooking the harbor it once defended. Design is simple with the remaining cannon mounted on tracks. Inside, it's overgrown with grass, and frigate birds soar overhead. It's a sharp drop to the deep blue sea below. A small crafts shop near the entrance sells bamboo, baskets, etc. Rusea's High School, founded by the French refugee in his will, is before the fort to the right. The parish church has an attractive steeple and cemetery. **others:** Lloyd is artist-in-residence at Gallery Hofstead. Try Club Canary for nightlife. Bustamante, who was Jamaica's only living national hero, was born in Blemyn, Hanover. At Bloody Bay, E of Negril, lies a nine-km stretch of totally undeveloped white sand beach. Ask the minibus driver to let you off. A beautiful view at Orange Bay.

stay: At the "Sandpiper," Church St., Edna McIntosh, a transplanted Canadian, offers accommodation for J$35 per rooms or d. Charlotte Inn Guest House, J$37 s, J$40 d, and West Palm Guest House, J$37 s, J$47 d, have the same owner; the difference is the latter has a fan and swimming pool. Also, try to rent a room or a bed from locals.

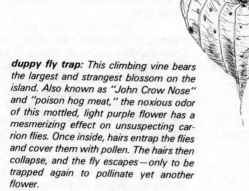

duppy fly trap: This climbing vine bears the largest and strangest blossom on the island. Also known as "John Crow Nose" and "poison hog meat," the noxious odor of this mottled, light purple flower has a mesmerizing effect on unsuspecting carrion flies. Once inside, hairs entrap the flies and cover them with pollen. The hairs then collapse, and the fly escapes—only to be trapped again to pollinate yet another flower.

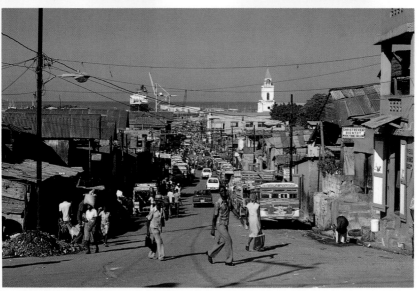

above, clockwise: street scene in Port-au-Prince (Harry S. Pariser); Baron Samedi and his consort Erzuli at Fete des Morts, Haiti (C.J. Marrow); Artist (Haitian National Office of Tourism); *Tap-Tap* in Port-au-Prince (Haitian National Office of Tourism)

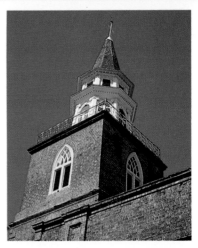

above, clockwise: Reach Falls, Portland Parish, Jamaica; Devon House, Kingston, Jamaica; Navy Island beach, Port Antonio, Jamaica; Cathedral Church of St. James, Spanish Town, Jamaica (all photos this page Harry S. Pariser)

HAITI

(REPUBLIQUE D'HAITI)

Often called "West Africa in the Caribbean," Haiti is a mixture of the cultures of West Africa, France, and Spain blended and revitalized. Through a long history of conflict and bloodshed, Haiti has always been uniquely Haiti, a republic 150 years before any African nation gained independence. Although much has been said about Haiti, the country remains the least understood, the most quixotic, enigmatic, and poorest nation in the Western Hemisphere. The color and contrast of Haitian life are reflected in its arts, including the paintings for which Haiti is so famous. Don't take things as they appear to be; look for the deeper meaning.

THE LAND

Haiti's 27,856 sq km (11,000 sq miles —roughly the size of Maryland) are squeezed onto the western third of the mountainous island of Hispaniola, second largest island in the Caribbean. Haiti shares a common 270-km (168-mile) border with the neighboring Dominican Republic. Cuba lies across the Windward Passage 90 km (56 miles) to the NW, Jamaica lies 180 km (112 miles) to the SW, and the Bahamas are a mere 112 km (70 miles) to the north. Haiti (derived from the native Indian name for the island, meaning "high land") is named appropriately because 40 percent of the land exceeds 450 m (1,500 ft.) in elevation. The primieval cover of tropical rainforest and Caribbean pine, which once blanketed the land, has been cleared—resulting in severe erosion problems. The land is semi-arid. The most extensive mountain system, the

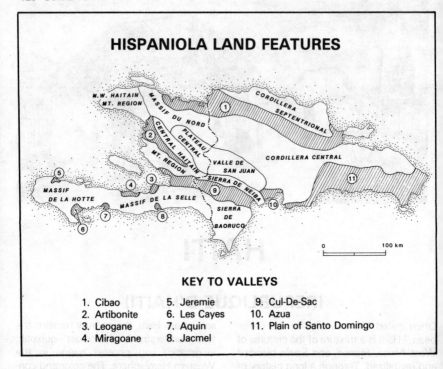

HISPANIOLA LAND FEATURES

KEY TO VALLEYS

1. Cibao
2. Artibonite
3. Leogane
4. Miragoane
5. Jeremie
6. Les Cayes
7. Aquin
8. Jacmel
9. Cul-De-Sac
10. Azua
11. Plain of Santo Domingo

Massif du Nord slants in a SE direction into the Dominican Republic, where it continues as the Cordillera Central. Satellite ranges at the western end of the island extend to the village of Le Mole-St. Nicholas at the NW tip. The Montagnes Noires, lying to the SW, are separated from the kindred Chaine de Mateaux, a range which extends into the Dominican Republic, by the Artibonite River. The eastern extension of this latter range, known as the Massif de la Selle, contains the Morne de la Selle, 2,734 m (8,793 ft.), highest mountain in the country. Agriculturally important lowlands cover 22 percent of the country. Once the heart of the country's sugar economy during the French colonial era and a geographical extension of Dominicana's

Valle du Cibao, the 388-sq-km (150-sq-mile) Plaine du Nord extends E from Cap Haitian to the Dominican border. To the S, the Plateau Centrale extends E from the Montagnes Noires to the Dominican border where it joins the Valle du San Juan. The 777-sq-km (300-sq-mile) Plaine de l'Artibonite is located N of the Chaine de Matreaux, and is separated from the Montagnes Noires. To the far S lies the 388-sq-km (150-sq-mile) Cul-de-Sac, a depression that meshes with the Neiba Valley in the Dominican Republic. More than 100 rivers and streams flow from the mountains down to the coast. With the exception of the longest, the Artibonite, they are short and steep. The other major rivers include the Troix Rivieres; the Grande Anse, the Massacre, and the

Pedernales. The latter two form portions of the Haitian-Dominican border. Brackish Etang Saumatre, located in the Cul-de-Sac near the Dominican border, is the largest lake. There are several small lakes and a reservoir, the Lac de Peligre. Largest offshore island is 207-sq-km (80-sq-mile) Gonave, located off Port-au-Prince. Ile de la Tortue, more commonly known by its Spanish name of Tortuga, lies off Port-de-Paix to the north.

climate: Fairly hospitable depending upon where you're going. There's not a whole lot of rain falling; no point receives more than 100 inches of rain. Port-au Prince is one of the hottest places in the country. Temperatures drop one degree F for every 275 feet of elevation. Hurricanes are infrequent.

flora and fauna: Insects are numerous with respect to the number of species; the time to see the many varieties of butterflies is in mid-summer. Land mammals are less numerous with the only indigenous species being the *agouti* (see "Fauna" under Jamaica). Vegetation is much the same as Jamaica's, with a variety of wild fruit trees, cactus, and red and grey mangroves present. Little remains of the forests which once covered the island.

cassava: *Once the staple crop of the Indian cultures of the Caribbean basin, the root is still a major food source, and cultivation has spread all over the world. It comes in two varieties: bitter and sweet. Bitter cassava is highly poisonous, but cooking prior to preparation renders it edible. The concentrated, milky juice which fills the roots is used as a basis for casareep and other Caribbean sauces, and cassava cakes and tapioca are made from the roots.*

HISTORY

discovery: Landing on the NW shore of the island in Dec. of legendary 1492, Columbus called it La Espanola—a fitting name for what was to become Spain's New World headquarters. Fort Navidad was constructed with timber from the Santa Maria, and a group of 30 men were left behind. When Columbus returned the following year, they were gone. After the sailors had enslaved native women and children—using them for sex and labor—the Indians retaliated by destroying their settlement. Focusing their attention on the gold found in the E, the Spanish ignored the W part of the island. Meanwhile, the native population was exterminated through forced labor and imported diseases, and blacks were brought over to slave in the gold mines in 1512.

French colonization: Tortuga (Tortue) Island off the N coast became a haven for buccaneers. From 1630-59 the island was intermittently controlled by the French, Spanish, English, and Dutch before finally winding up in French hands. Fort Margot, established in 1641 on the W coast of the island, was placed under the control of the French West Indies Com-

pany in 1664. The western third of Hispaniola was ceded to France in 1697 under the treaty of Ryswick; it was named Sainte-Dominique and eventually became France's richest overseas colony. Exports included raw and white sugar, coffee, high-quality cacao, rum, molasses, tobacco, and hides. By 1790, total imports and exports exceeded those of the U.S. or exports of all of Spain's colonies combined. In 1685 Louis XIV issued a decree which freed certain *gens de couleur* (colored persons). A total of 28,000 of these mulattoes, together with 36,000 whites, oversaw half a million slaves. Abuse of these slaves was common. One report had it that a French planter nailed a slave to the wall by his ears, sliced them off, grilled them, and made the other slaves eat them.

the Haitian revolution: Although the liberated mulattoes (*affranchis*) had been made citizens, and the French Revolution had resulted in the abolition of slavery and a directive to restore full civil rights to all *gens de couleur,* they were denied their full civil rights through restrictive laws passed by the white planters. Leaders of a mulatto revolt were executed in March 1791, and the slaves revolted a few months later. A massacre two years later took the lives of all whites who didn't flee the island. Although the French sent in 6,000 troops, they were repulsed, and slavery was officially abolished in 1793. One of the leaders of the slave revolt, Toussaint L'Ouverture, assumed dictatorial powers. His 1801 constitution declared the entire island to be an independent nation and granted himself the status of president for life — a status, however, which didn't last long. Napoleon, seeking to keep Haiti as a supply base for his conquest of N. America, sent a 23,000-man expeditionary force to subdue the revolt. Although Toussaint died in a French prison in 1803, the French were forced to surrender in Dec. of that same year to Gen. Jean-Jacques Dessalines, who in turn proclaimed Haiti's independence on 1 Jan. 1804.

post-independence Haiti: After Dessalines' assassination in 1806, Henri Cristophe set up a kingdom in the N and ruled from 1806-20, while Alexandre Petion, a French-educated mulatto, set up a republic in the S from 1806-18. Reuniting the N and S after Cristophe's suicide in 1820, Jean Pierre Boyer also annexed the Spanish portion of Hispaniola. In exchange for France's recognition of Haiti's independent status, Boyer pledged a 150-million-franc indemnity which crippled Haiti's economy for decades thereafter. Ousted by a coup d'etat in 1843, Boyer was replaced by a string of successors. There were 22 different presidents between 1849-1915, and between 1908-15 alone, there were seven presidents and 20 uprisings.

the American intervention: In 1915, the growing concerns among American investors stemming from the unstable political climate, coupled with rumors

This cartoon, "The Missionary," which appeared in the Marines Magazine *in April 1917, illustrates the attitude of the occupying forces toward the Haitian people.*

that Germany was seeking to establish a naval base there, prompted President Woodrow Wilson to order the Marines to intervene in Haiti. Retaining control of the country until 1934, the Marines collected customs duties, directed public projects, and organized a national guard which evolved into the modern Haitian army. The Marines also suppressed an uprising by the *cacos* — mercenary guerrillas who had placed many Haitian leaders in power in return for a suitable sum and the opportunity to loot towns along the way to the capital. The American intervention changed nothing. Although Stenio Vincent, a mulatto, was elected president in 1930, political instability continued unabated. Mulattoes ruled the country until 1946, when Dumarsais Estime, who was placed in power by black leaders that year, purged the government of mulatto officials. Estime was sent into exile by the military in 1950 when he tried to change the constitution so that he could succeed himself. He was followed by Col. Paul E. Magloire, a powerful army official overthrown in Dec. 1956. After a series of seven shaky governments, Francois Duvalier was elected president in Sept. 1957.

THE DUVALIER ERA

Despite his soft-spoken demeanor, Francois Duvalier, popularly known as "Papa Doc," proved himself a man to be reckoned with. Self-described as the first Haitian president to have "a pen in one hand and a gun in the other," this compact, five-and-a-half-foot, 150-pound man—son of a justice of the peace—was a demon in disguise. A physician-ethnologist by trade and an astute student of Machiavelli, Duvalier compared himself with Dessalines, Mao Tse-tung, Ataturk, Charles de Gaulle, and Christ. With his black suit and hat and heavy black plastic spectacles, Duvalier was taken by the peasantry to be a living incarnation of Voodoo *loa* Baron Samedi—a resemblance Duvalier was quick to take advantage of. A Voodoo *houngan,* many believed him to be a *bocor* as well. Duvalier had dominated the post-WW II movement, which was led by a small black elite, and evolved into his ideology of *negritude:* the transference of power from the mulatto elite to the blacks. Swiftly eliminating his rivals, Duvalier's next move was to gain complete control over the military. By 1958, the *Tonton Macoutes,* symbol of the Duvalier regime, had emerged. (The name *Tonton Macoute* means "Uncle Knapsack" in Haitian Creole; the original *Tonton Macoute* is the antithesis of *Tonton Noel.* Good children receive Christmas presents from *Tonton Noel* while the naughty ones are swiftly plunged into the depths of *Tonton Macoute's* knapsack, never to be seen again.) Drawn from the slums of Port-au-Prince and dressed in blue serge suits and sunglasses, these officers of *Tonton Macoute* were enrolled by Papa Doc himself. Relying on extortion, their mission was to snuff out any opposition that might pose a danger to the regime. The *Tonton Macoute* (now renamed the *Volontaries de la Securite Nationale*) were supplemented by the *Police Secrete,* the *Milice Civile,* the elite *Garde Presidentiel,* and the loyal *Batalion Dessalines,* which served to counterbalance potentially hostile elements in the military.

President for Life: In the 1961 legislative elections, held two years before his presidential term expired, Duvalier had his name printed at the top of the ballot. Although only an estimated 100,000 voted, the government announced that 1,320,000 ballots had been cast, all of Duvalier's deputies had been elected, and—to everyone's surprise as no one had known he was running—Francois Duvalier had been elected to another six-year term! In 1964, in a forthright move designed to banish forever such bothersome oddities as elections, the legislature adopted a new constitution proclaiming Papa Doc to be *presidente-a-vie de la republique* (president for life). In the plebescite which followed, exactly 2,800,000 Haitians voted "oui" while 3,234 voted "non." The latter were arrested and charged with defacing ballots. American aid was

suspended in 1962 and formally curtailed in 1963. By the mid-'60s, about 80 percent of Haiti's professionals had fled to America, the U.S., and Canada. Corruption was rife. Funds ostensibly collected for building public facilities were diverted toward paying the salaries of the security forces and creating a series of enormous neon signs in Port-au-Prince which declared such profound Duvalier thoughts as "I have no enemies save the enemy of the country," and "I am the Haitian flag, one and indivisible."

Although there was no lack of opposition to Duvalier during the 1960s, no one—not even the CIA—was able to unseat him. Attempted invasions mounted by Haitians residing abroad were farcically unsuccessful. Early in 1971, Duvalier, his health failing, announced that he had picked his son Jean-Claude to succeed him. A proposition to that effect was passed by the voters by 2,391,916 to zero. On 21 April 1971, Francois "Papa Doc" left this planet.

GOVERNMENT

Just as the Haitian lower classes remained oriented to African culture, so the elite, ironically, tended to espouse the values and culture of 19th C. France. Although the French and the American revolutions had their impact upon the nation's way of thinking, the autocratic model, with which they had firsthand experience, dominated. Notably, the three earliest Haitian leaders (L'Ouverture, Dessalines, Cristophe) modeled themselves after none other than

Napoleon Bonaparte. The Napoleonic model, in which a demagogue fulfills his fantasies, is one which has come to life in Haiti, and it continues to bedevil the country today. Unlike revolutions elsewhere, the benefits of the Haitian Revolution were reaped chiefly by the elite. Because the peasant has come to associate the government only with taxes and conscription, he has always shunned political participation. Therefore, the peasant poses little political or social threat. Consequently, it's easy for the elite to pretend to ignore the peasant's lot. It is not difficult to exercise effective social control over a group of illiterates living at the subsistence level. Accustomed to generation upon generation of being stepped on, the peasant has adopted a stoic pessimism which befits Haiti's moribund political climate. Nationalism in Haiti is a concept reserved for the elite. In an autocracy where only one president (Stenio Vincent, in 1941) has been followed by a democratically elected successor, the chief problem facing the executive branch is how to prolong its longevity.

political structure: On the surface the Haitian Constitution appears to contain a system with checks and balances; unfortunately, it has always been treated more as an ordinary piece of paper than as a binding charter. The Duvaliers have been among the worst offenders. The most recent Haitian Constitution, promulgated on 27 Aug. 1983, replaced Papa Doc's 1964 version. The *Chambre Legislative* (National Assembly) is a 59-member unicameral body whose deputies are "elected" for six-year terms. Meeting for only three months each year, the president-for-life "is endowed with full powers to pass decrees having force of law" for the remaining nine months. It has also been the custom to suspend certain constitutional rights—such as the right to assemble, the right to form unions, protection against house search, prohibition of illegal arrests and detentions—during the recess period. The president also personally appoints all members of the judiciary. The last free elections were held in 1957. There have never been political parties in the true sense in Haiti; parties have always tended

to focus on one leader. Under the Duvaliers, only one party and one leader have been tolerated. Sylvio Claude, leader and founder of the opposition PDCH (the Haitian Christian Democratic Party) has spent most of the last six years in prison, under house arrest, or in hiding. In 1984, Jean-Claude Duvalier banned all parties save his ruling *Parti Unique de l'Action Revolutionaire et Gouvernementale.*

the Jean-Claude Duvalier days: Although initially thought to present a reformist image, "Baby Doc" has followed steadfastly in the shadow of his father, continuing on the path of autocratic rule which leaves the great mass of the Haitian people disenfranchised and very much divorced from the political decision-making. On 27 May 1984, Jean-Claude married Michele Bennet at the Croix de Banquets presidential ranch in a US$6 million ceremony. In 1980, in celebration of Reagan's election and the consequent removal of the onerous evil eye of human rights placed there by the Carter administration, all leading journalists and political dissidents were arrested. Anxious to strengthen his anti-Cuba front, Reagan soon moved to strengthen ties. Since they could be considered to be little other than a shell game anyway, it came as no surprise that the 59 legislators, elected by vast majorities in the 12 Feb. 1984 elections, were all "dedicated Jean-Claudistes" (to use the government's description). In the village of Petit-Gonave, Gerard Nelson was declared the winner in the morning; in the afternoon, however, the victory was awarded to Jean Sassine—a friend of Jean-Claude's father-in-law. Riots broke out after the new results were announced, but they were quelled quickly.

ECONOMY

One of the most backward of the world's economies, Haiti ranks as the 29th poorest nation on earth. So desperate is Haiti's plight that hundreds of thousands of Haitians have chosen to risk the perils of migration by sea rather than face continued hardship at home. (An estimated 40,000 illegally migrated from 1979-1982 alone.) Although the U.S. has pumped approximately US$100 million in aid into the country, most of this has gone to fill the Duvalier family coffers or to pay for the extensive paramilitary infrastructure. The only public works that may be pointed to is the Peligre Dam at the headwaters of the Artibonite River, and some major roads; otherwise, the record is bleak. Although the Haitian GNP is said to give workers a per capita income of US$270 per year, the fact is that about 60 percent of all Haitians have less than US$60 per year to live on. Meanwhile, five percent of the population has control over 50 percent of the national income. Of the approximately 4,000 families that are believed to earn US$90,000 or above, 75 percent live in Port-au-Prince. They pay taxes amounting to three percent of their incomes, and their money is invested abroad where it receives higher rates. This overseas investment means a drain on the economy as well as a lack of funds for investment and development of the infrastructure Haiti so badly needs. (Jean-Claude Duvalier alone is estimated to have US$400 million stashed in foreign banks.)

foreign investment: Largest investor is the United States. Reasons for the U.S. presence are threefold: Haitian labor is cheap and strike-free (unions are non-existent); American companies are offered up to 15 years of tax-exempt status; and a large number of goods are allowed entry duty-free to the U.S. market. American firms employ approximately 60,000 workers at an unenforced minimum wage of US$2.64 *per day* — significantly more than the average Haitian wage but still well under the U.S. minimum of US$3.35 per hour. American companies are more than eager to exploit this wage level, and many are switching operations from the more expensive Far East (where they may have to pay workers as much as US$1.20 per hour) to Haiti with its more profitable hourly wage of US$0.33. Items manufactured in Haiti include shoes, undergarments, sportswear, beaded accessories, stitching of baseballs and softballs, toys, and simple electronic components. U.S. companies investing in Haiti range from CBS, Inc., which manufactures Sesame Street stuffed animals, to Gulf and Western, which manufactures blue jeans and flannel shirts. Now the world's largest producer of baseballs, Haiti's seven plants produce hundreds of thousands of balls annually. While the material to make baseballs is the largest non-agricultural import from the U.S., baseballs are Haiti's largest U.S.-bound export.

agriculture: Although primary agricultural products form the bulk of exports and 90 percent of the population tills the soil, the sad fact is that Haiti is a net importer of agricultural goods. Haiti's agriculture is still very much at the subsistence level, and agricultural productivity is declining at the rate of two percent per year. After independence, the struggles for which had largely destroyed the plantation system, the land was divided up into small plots and divided among the peasantry. As the government required that all inherited plots be divided equally among the male children, the plots have shrunk accordingly over generations. Today, the vast majority of the 560,000 farms cover five acres or less. Methods employed in cultivation are usually very primitive. All cultivation is by hoe and/or machete (the plow is unknown); slash-and-burn cultivation, responsible for erosion which has helped denude the soil, is still used. Coffee—of low quality and yield—is the main cash crop, while maize, beans, rice, plantains, yams, millet, and sorghum are the main crops grown for food. Haitian peasants were struck another blow in the past few years. In an all-out extermination campaign conducted by Haitian authorities, the Haitian pig population, which formerly numbered some 400,000, has dwindled to nearly nought. The U.S. dispensed US$22 million for this campaign because a small number of the porkers had been found infected with swine fever—a disease which, if it were to spread, would have caused grunts of disconcertment from America's $10 billion hog industry.

other sectors: Although the mining of bauxite contributes eight percent of Haiti's GNP, it employs less than a thousand people. Tourism, hampered by the stigma of AIDS (Acquired Immune Deficiency Syndrome) and Haiti's negative image abroad, is less important than in other Caribbean economies. Haiti's liberal divorce laws have, however, succeeded in luring tourists. One lucrative racket (for those who control it) is that of blood plasma export. For one or two pints of blood, poor Haitians receive US$4 and a bottle of soda pop.

current economic situation: With a tradition of self-serving, introspective, and elitist government, Haiti has always had severe economic problems. Haiti's trade balance has been continually in arrears since 1960. Its economic situation is nothing short of desperate, and Haiti has been placed in the category reserved for the poorest of the poor Third World nations: that of a Fourth World nation. The largest increases have been in basic food imports which comprise 30 percent of all imports. On 29 May 1984 in the town of Gonaives, government troops killed 10 civilians in food riots which resulted after food distributed by CARE was being sold rather than given away.

RELIGION

VOODOO

Without a doubt, no religion in the world has been so misunderstood and vilified as Voodoo. The syncretistic religion, cousin of similar ones spread from New Orleans to Brazil, has been unfairly portrayed as a religion of bloody sacrifices and pagan rituals. In actuality, Voodoo is a complex reblending of African religious beliefs with elements of Christianity thrown in for good measure. Voodoo comes from a Dahomnean word meaning "god," but it cannot be identified with any particular African tribe. Although found elsewhere in the Americas, it has reached its highest level of sophistication and influence in Haiti. Voodoo (or *vodun* in Haiti) is as intimately intertwined with Haitian history, society, and culture as its cousin Catholicism is in Italy. As the saying goes, Haiti is 90 percent Catholic and 100 percent Voodoo. This is actually an exaggeration; less than a third of all Hai-

tians are staunch Catholics; the vast majority are peasants practicing a Catholicism laden with Voodoo. Voodoo is an informal, living religion which provides the Haitian peasant with a way to deal on a mediatory basis with the spiritual forces of the universe. As is the case with many other religions, Voodoo establishes codes of behavior. And Voodoo ceremonies serve to increase family solidarity. A subject of continual controversy and conflict, Voodoo has been attacked by the elite in public while being practiced by them in private. Voodoo has been repressed under the American occupation, or under the regime of elite mulatto President Lescot in the 1940s, but it has always made a comeback. Duvalier cleverly utilized Voodoo as a means of social control, and even elevated a Voodoo priest to the status of secretary of state.

pantheon: There are over 1,000 spirits in the Voodoo pantheon; the Haitian words for deity, *loa* or *mystere,* derive from the Yoruba word *l'awo,* meaning mystery. *Loas* come in all shapes and sizes; they may reside in special caves, trees, waterfalls, springs, and stones. While predominantly from the Kongo and Angola, Haiti's slave population was also brought from the Dahomney, Yoruba, Bamana, Mande, and Igbo territories in W. Africa. Haitian Voodoo is primarily a synthesis of the Dahomney, Yoruba, and Kongo religious traditions: its pantheon reflects this, as well as the considerable influence of Catholicism. Spirits are grouped into two categories or sides: *Rada* and *Petro-Lemba.* While *Rada* is named after slaves brought from Rada on Dohomney's (now Benin's) coast, *Petro-Lemba* (or *Petra*) is named after a compound formed by combining the name of a messianic figure from Haiti's SW peninsula with the name of a northern Kongo trading and healing society. While the *Rada* team of spirits—predominantly Dahomnean and Yoruba in origin—are considered to be largely "cool" or "civilian" and associated with achieving peace and reconciliation, the *Petro* group are "hot" or "military," thought to be ag-

gressive and even ferocious. Largely Kongo in origin, they are usually associated with the spiritual charms for healing and for attacking evil forces. Many *Petro loa* are local in origin. Cousin Zaca is the *loa* of agriculture; Baron Samedi, who lives in cemeteries and traffics in the souls of the dead, was often associated—to the advantage of the latter—with the late great Papa Doc. Slaves coming in contact with Catholicism were swift to note the similarities—superficial or misconstrued though they might be—between the *loas* and the saints. Virgin Mary has been equated with Maitresse Erzulie, goddess of love; St. George riding a charger is seen as Ogun Badagris, god of war. While this may disturb the pious priests, it seems natural enough to the pantheistic Haitians.

places of worship: Bearing distinct similarities in terms of spatial relationship to similar compounds in Central and W. Africa, *Houmforts,* the religious centers of *vodun,* have as their focus the *peristyle.* This dancing area, usually covered with a straw roof, has as its focal point the *poteau mitan* or "center post."

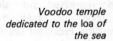

Voodoo temple dedicated to the loa *of the sea*

Used as the fulcrum for dances or ground paintings, deities either ascend (from the watery regions below) or descend (from the heavens above). Adjacent to the *houmfort* stands a building with rooms containing altars or *pe*. Each is dedicated to particular spirits and displays an incredibly eclectic array of bric-a-brac including numerous bottles and containers, thunder-stones (Arawak Axeheads), rattles, and other ritual objects.

services: While black magic is (at least officially) the province of the *bocor* or sorcerer who dispenses charms and amulets and may invoke a curse, the *houngan* (Voodoo priest), and *mambo* (Voodoo priestess), interpret and serve the *loa*. As is the case with Catholic saints, however, *loas* act as intermediaries between a creator busily occupied with weighty matters and the lowly human being. Unlike the Catholic saints, *loas* prove their existence by possessing the *hounsis* or initiates. The beginning of a ceremony is marked by the drawing of the *veve* (ritual drawing with corn flour or ashes). Derived from a merger of different African ground designs coupled with a touch of indigenous Haitian ingenuity, the *veve* is the family crest of the particular *loa* and serves to call it. (By tradition, Legba, a spirit who guards gateways and crossroads, is usually invoked first because without his permission other gods could not enter the temple.) As the

loa enters the scene, he mounts his *choual* (horse), and the *choual* is seized with violent convulsions which can last anywhere from several minutes to a few hours. Possession by a *loa* means that the *choual* may exhibit the characteristics of the deity. For example, while under the influence of the serpent god Damballa, a man may seem to glide up a tree like a serpent. After an individual is first mounted by a *loa*, he is baptized in the name of that particular *loa* and will pay homage to him throughout his lifetime. After death, the *loa* is removed so that the man's soul may ascend upward to reside with the Christian God. Voodoo ceremonies usually involve sacrifice of animals, including doves, pigs, chickens, turkeys, goats, sheep, and an occasional

Dancer in Voodoo dance show at a hotel in Petionville. As it is difficult for the visitor to see an authentic voodoo ceremony, a tourist-oriented show like this may be the best one can do.

bull. There is no concrete evidence that "the goat without horns" was ever sacrificed, although human sacrifices were part of ceremonial tradition of late 19th C. Dahomney. It's rare for a visitor to see an authentic Voodoo ceremony; most of those open to non-initiates are staged for money.

zombies: A longstanding Haitian tradition, Zombieism was not given much credence until recently. According to tradition, zombies (*zombis*) are men or women who, having transgressed the laws of the community or gone against the family will, are drugged into a trance-like state, buried, and then dug up after burial and taken off to work as slaves. Support for the existence of zombies has recently been documented by Harvard botanist E. Wade Davies who, together with Dr. Lamarque Douyon (head of the Psychiatric Center in Port-au-Prince), has discovered the root of the legend. According to them, zombies are fed a coma-inducing drug made from a combination of a large toad and one or more species of puffer fish. The toad contains a variety of hallucinogens, powerful anesthetics and chemicals that affect the heart and nervous system; the fish contains a deadly nerve poison called tetrodotoxin. Although it remains a mystery how zombies are revived, it is known that they must be revived within an eight-hour period. After revival, they are force-fed a pate of sweet potato and datura. Known locally as zombie-cucumber, datura is one of the strongest known hallucinogenic plants. Caught in a psychedelic stupor, the zombie is then led away to work as a slave.

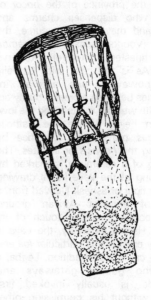

FESTIVALS AND EVENTS

Appropriately enough, the Haitian calendar of events opens with *Jou d'Lan,* or New Year's, which is also Haiti's Independence Day. All promenade about wearing their new clothes, and wreaths and flowers are placed at the statue of the unknown Maroon in Port-au-Prince. Forefather's Day (2 Jan.) is marked by a personal appearance by the president-for-life; sandwiched between a cavalcade of Mercedes limos (which race through the streets, turn corners sharply and stop for nothing), Jean-Claude Duvalier throws out fistfuls of five-gourde notes to the assembled citizenry. Rehearsals for Carnival take place every Sunday from the first Sunday after New Year's annually. Groups of people in costume parade through the streets in the company of marching bands, some of whose members play the *vaccine* (an instrument made from a hollow bamboo tube); also present are *lamayotes,* small boxes containing a pet animal, carried by boys. Mardi Gras, held the Tuesday before Lent, marks the last day of Carnival. It is during this time of year that the *rara,* a group dance which derives historically from long vanished 15th and 16th C. European traditions, comes into play. It takes place between the end of Carnival and Easter. Every day, beginning Palm Sunday, dancers, wearing red shirts and carrying red flags, come down from the hills early in the morning and will dance for the public in return for small sums. Some may carry a dead chicken or rooster on a stick; others carry kerosene lanterns; still others play *vaccines* or drums. Their leader is usually dressed like a jester with a silver sequined and colored vest, baton, and colored handkerchiefs.

When they happen to meet, bands may challenge each other to competitive dances. During this time, wrestlers hold exhibitions near Jeremie. On 1 May, Agriculture and Labor Day, produce is exhibited at the School of Agriculture in Port-au-Prince. On 16 July, a ceremony called the *saut d'eau* is held at the village of Ville-Bonheur. Commemorating the miraculous appearance of a virgin in a tree near a waterfall, the ceremony indiscriminately mixes the Voodoo and Catholic pantheon. One of the four biggest holidays is *Fete des Morts* (All Souls Day). On this day (2 Nov.), some people offer food to their ancestors. Called *Manger aux Morts* ("Food for the Dead"), the food may be placed on the ground or at the place at the table where the deceased used to eat; there, a candle is lit and prayers are said. *Manger-yam,* a two-day Voodoo-oriented harvest festival, is

held in November. Christmas, the last holiday of the year, is also one of the most elaborate. On Christmas Eve children carry *fanals* (churches or houses constructed from cardboard strips with candles or kerosene lamps inside) down from the mountains. Bamboo or palm-thatched, arch-shaped shelters known as *tonelles,* which may be used as a shelter or as a dancing place, are decorated with strips of colored paper and gourds. Festivities include the stringing of elaborate displays of lights in Port-au-Prince and street dances. Secular events—such as birthdays and weddings—are celebrated by the *bamboche* (spree). The *combite* is a communal working party of Haitians who work and drink *clairin* to the beat of drums; a dance may follow the *combite* and run late into the night.

FESTIVALS AND EVENTS

1 Jan.:	Independence Day/New Year's Day
2 Jan.:	Forefather's Day/Heroes' Day
Feb./Mar.:	Carnival or Mardi Gras (3 days before Ash Wednesday)
14 April:	Pan American Day
April:	Ascension (moveable)
18 May:	Flag Day/University Day
22 May:	Sovereignty Day
May:	Corpus Christi (movable)
22 June:	Birthday of the President for Life
15 August:	Assumption Day
17 Oct.:	Dessalines' Death Anniversary
24 Oct.:	U.N. Day
1 Nov.:	All Saints' Day
18 Nov.:	Armed Forces Day
5 Dec.:	Discovery Day
25 Dec.:	Christmas Day

PRACTICALITIES

getting there: The border with the Dominican Republic is closed; entry into Haiti is limited to air (commercial airlines) or sea (private craft). American Airlines and Air Haiti fly from New York City; Eastern, Air France, and Air Florida fly direct from Miami. Air Canada flies nonstop from Montreal. ALM flies direct from New York City, Miami, Kingston and San Juan. Air Jamaica flies twice weekly from Kingston and San Juan.

getting around: Can be difficult. There are only 960 km of paved roads in the country. The best roads run from Port-au-Prince to Jacmel, Les Cayes, and to Cap Haitien. Many villages are accessible only by foot path, and many roads are impassable during the rainy season. The railway network has died from neglect. Buses do run between Port-au-Prince and Cap Haitien. Otherwise, jumbo-sized versions of the *tap-tap camions* (colorfully painted trucks) transport cargo and passengers between cities. All-inclusive rates for car rentals start from US$28 per day. Internal flights (from Port-au-Prince) to Jacmel, Cap Haitien, Jeremie, Les Cayes, and Port-au-Paix are provided by Air Inter and Turks and Caicos airways.

accommodations: Within the budget range, a variety of accommodation is available. The cheaper hotels may be geared for prostitutes. Be sure to see if there is running water and toilet facilities before moving into one. Higher-priced hotels charge in US$ and add a 10-percent service charge, along with a five-percent government tax. In the rural areas, stay with missionaries.

food: A large number of local restaurants in the urban areas. A staple meal at a local restaurant (about G0.12) consists of rice and beans, boiled bananas, and a piece of meat or fish. Haitian delicacies include *djon djon* (rice, lima beans, and black mushrooms), *timalice* (an onion and herb concoction), and *calalou,* the usual Caribbean stew. Tap water is never safe to drink; the main hotels provide carafes of boiled water. *Clarin* is the local rough rum; Babancourt is the favorite of the elite. Because of its high cost, many locals must forego rice in favor of *mai malu* (ground corn) and *piti-mi* (sorghum).

market near Petionville

money: A rather confusing situation. After the Marines' departure in 1934, the gourde was set at a five-to-one parity. In reality, you can receive slightly more than this at the very open black market which lines Rue Dessalines in downtown Port-au-Prince. One gourde is divided into 100 centimes. There are coins of 5, 10, 20, 50 centimes *(kob)* and notes of 1, 2, 5, 10, 20, 50, 100, 250, and 500 gourdes. However, American coinage is also in use so it's possible to give and receive change in both currencies, and prices may be listed in either currency. The important thing to keep straight is that the ratio is five to one, so one must keep dividing or multiplying by five. Banks are open Mon. to Fri. 0900-1300. Be sure to carry plenty of change at all times because *tap-tap* drivers and others may be reluctant to return it.

visas: U.S. and Canadians must have proof of citizenship (birth certificate, voter's registration, passport), plus an ongoing ticket. Citizens of Britain, Austria, Belgium, Denmark, W. Germany, Netherlands, Switzerland, Luxembourg, and Israel are required to have a passport and ongoing ticket. All others need passports and visas.

conduct: The fact that a large number of Haitians want or expect something material from you can be rather trying at times. If hassled unduly by beggars, touts, or guides, just say, *"Moin pas gain l'argent"* ("I don't have much money").

Moneychangers line Rue Dessalines in Port-au-Prince.

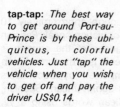

tap-tap: *The best way to get around Port-au-Prince is by these ubiquitous, colorful vehicles. Just "tap" the vehicle when you wish to get off and pay the driver US$0.14.*

They won't believe you, but they'll get the point that they're not going to get anything out of you.

health: Health services are abysmal. Note, however, that AIDS can only be spread by contact with infected blood or sex; Haitians have been found to be no more at risk than any other group, so there is no undue need for concern. Typhoid innoculations are recommended. If planning to travel outside of Port-au-Prince, begin taking malaria tablets two weeks before arrival and be sure to bring water purification tablets with you.

measurements: U.S., metric, and other systems are in use. The *aune* (47 in.) is an old French measure that, outside of Haiti, survives only in Switzerland and Belgium. Another, even more eclectic, measure is the *marmite,* a four to five pound cooking pot, which is further divided into *godets* (bowls). Land is measured in *careau* (units of 3.33 acres). There are 12 measures for coffee and 17 for cacao.

theft: In a country where one may receive a six-month jail sentence for taking the name of the *president-a-vie* in vain, the average Haitian doesn't mess around with stealing things. Severe punishment and abhorrent jail conditions and an intensive intelligence network (combining the police, military, and paramilitary) serve as a deterrent to crime. Thus, Haiti may have the lowest crime rate in the Americas.

services and information: While in Port-au-Prince, obtain the free *News of Haiti.* Mail inside the country can take months. Electric service is unreliable. An old Haitian joke maintains that you can't get the number you want on the phone unless you know what wrong number to call!

shopping: Haiti has a colorful if repetitive craft scene. Most famous of all are the paintings. Although those by famous artists may fetch prices reaching into the thousands of dollars, the average paintings fit more into the line of the color-by-numbers school of painting and seem to have been turned *en masse* off an assembly line. Nowadays, Haitian crafts are specifically for the tourist market. Other crafts include carved wooden goods, embroidered clothing, and copper jewelry. The Iron Market is the cheapest place to shop, and all tourist shops are higher priced. Shops are open Mon. to Fri. 0800-1700 summer and winter; Sat. from 0800-1200, closed Sundays. All essential items are imported by higglers and priced accordingly.

broadcasting and media: There are 21 commercial radio stations and two television stations. More than a half-century ago, newspapers were seen as being daily pamphlets for or against the government. Today, the only thing that has changed is that only the government broadside appears. Of the five daily newspapers, *Le Matin* is controlled by the Duvalier clan, and tacit censorship keeps the others in line.

language: Although approximately 10 percent of the population speak Parisian French, the language of the country is really Creole. Creole is a mixture of Norman French (imported by buccaneers some 500 years ago), African, Spanish, and native Antillean words using a W. African syntax. Although Creole and French are mutually unintelligible, Creole wasn't recognized as an official language until 1969. Many young people in Port-au-Prince and most of the elite speak English. The average peasant speaks very little French and no English.

HAITI NATIONAL OFFICES OF TOURISM

Chicago
919 North Michigan Avenue
Suite 3311
Chicago, Illinois 60611
tel. (312) 337-1603

Miami, Florida
150 South East 2nd Avenue
Republic Bank Building
Suite 1013
Miami, Florida, 33131
tel. (305) 371-9420

New Orleans, Louisiana
(Consulate)
611 Common Street
Suite 602
New Orleans, LA 70130
tel. (504) 568-8309

San Juan Puerto Rico
P.O. Box 3761
San Juan, Puerto Rico 00936
tel. (809) 753-0825

New York City
Haiti National Office of Tourism
1270 Avenue of the Americas
New York, New York 10020
tel. (212) 757-3517

Washington DC
2311 Massachusetts Avenue NW.
Washington DC 20008
tel. (202) 328-1888

Montreal, Canada
44 Fundy, Etage F
Casier Postal 187
Place Bonaventure
Montreal, Canada H5A 1A9
tel. (514) 871-9897

Toronto, Ontario, Canada
(Consulate)
113 Simonston Boulevard
Toronto L3X 4L9
Ontario, Canada
tel. (416) 886-3398

PORT-AU-PRINCE

INTRODUCTION

Undoubtedly the dustiest and dirtiest capital city in the Third World, Port-au-Prince is certain to have its effect on you; you'll either love it or loathe it. It's a city of crowded, filthy streets with an almost overwhelming cacophony of humanity, and cornucopia of often smoldering garbage. The streets teem with people and colorfully painted *tap-taps;* women wearing colorful scarves sell peanut brittle, fruit, and cigarettes. With a population of 700,000, Port-au-Prince remains the only modern city in the country, and one which dominates the political, economic, and social scene as well. Laid out in an area which resembles a roughly hewn triangle, the tip is located where the fertile Cul-de-Sac plain emerges from the mountains overlooking the gulf. Along the E and NE of the city, buildings line the foothills of the 1,100 ft. Gros Morne while

the SW area of the city is spread over the slopes of Morne l'Hopital, which rises to 3,500 feet.

history: Anchoring in 1706 at the foot of Morne l'Hopital, the captain of the ship *Prince* christened the bay "Port-au-Prince." Renaming it Port Royal in 1738, Governor de Fayet chose it as the new colonial capital. Fort Ilet, a 12-gun battery, was built on l'Ilet du Prince, and the town was proclaimed capital of Sainte-Domingue in 1749. Every building in town was leveled by the 1770 earthquake. The city burned during the revolution in 1791, and was renamed Port Republicain during the Spanish occupation of 1793-94. The British took Port-au-Prince on 4 June 1794 and evacuated the town—teaving it to Toussaint—on 4 June 1797. The French invaded and occupied Port-au-Prince in Feb. 1802, and Dessalines drove them out in March 1804. Simon Bolivar found a hospitable refuge in Port-au-Prince for four months in 1816. Fires swept the city in 1820, 1822, and 1865-66. The army sacked the city in May 1868, and the city burned again in 1871, 1872, 1873, 1883, and 1908. The National Palace was destroyed in 1912 after a cache of dynamite secreted in the basement exploded. A touristic fiasco (poorly planned, mismanaged, and underpatronized), the 1949-50 $6 million International Exposition was held in Port-au-Prince.

arriving by air: Immigration will stamp your passport for up to a three-month stay. Customs are efficient; the tourist information center is straight ahead. The exchange booth is often closed, so have US$0.14 ready for the *tap-tap* fare to town; all *tap-taps* run the 13 km into Blvd. J.J. Dessalines, the main street. Fare-regulated taxis also run to the tourist hotels.

getting around: Can be confusing because of language and currency difficulties (see main "Introduction"). *Tap-taps* are the local bus service. Just tap the vehicle when you wish to get off and pay US$0.14. More expensive are the *camionettes*. These station wagons or minibuses usually reach outside the city and charge US$0.25. Ancient sedans which stop at requested locations, *taxi-publiques* can be identified by their red kerchiefs attached to their windscreens. They charge US$0.30.

guides: An inevitable feature of Port-au-Prince street life, you will be accosted at every street corner by aspiring guides. While having one will keep the others at bay, you will have to provide food and may end up paying higher prices for purchases. On the other hand, a guide can help you find your bearings and take you to some out-of-the way destinations. In any case, it may be easier to go along with the system and pay them US$2-3 per day to take you around than to try to do without. What few things there are to be seen in the city may easily be reached on foot. Walking around the outer parts of town—even for those accustomed to life in the Third World—can be a fascinating experience.

SIGHTS

Place des Heros de l'Independence (Champ de Mars): This large park and recreation center features public concerts regularly. Statues of former Haitian rulers Dessalines, Petion, and Henri Cristophe line Place de Heros de l'Independence. Nearby are Musee de Pantheon National (US$3 admission), Musee Defly (a restored gingerbread mansion), and Musée d'Art Haitian du College St. Pierre. Located along Rue Capois, the latter supports a good collection of early primitives. Located to the N of Blvd. J.J. Dessalines, the famous statue of the Marron Inconnu, a bronze portrayal of the unknown slave who blew the conch shell calling for the assembly of independent troops, is the focal point. In the background is the gleaming white Palais National. Built in 1918, it was modeled after the U.S. Capitol Building. The yellow building to the right of the palace is the Francois Duvalier barracks. Also known as "Casernes Dessalines," it is one of the city's largest buildngs. Reports received by Amnesty International allege that torture takes place inside its walls. Near the end of Rue Capois off Rue Cadet Jeremie stands the legendary Oloffson street; Castera Bazile painted the Ascension, and Riguad Benoit produced the Virgin and Child. Wilson Bigaud's "The Marriage of Cana" has a policeman chasing a chicken thief in one corner. Jasmin Joseph sculpted the ceramic choir screen in 1954 as a memorial to groundbreaking Haitian painter Hector Hyppolite. A small shop, across the street from the side door exit, sells paintings. Other cathedrals include La Cathedrale Notre Dame and l'Ancienne Cathedrale, which was built by the French in 1920.

Musee National: Near Bois Patete off Ave. John Brown (usually open Mon. to Fri., 0830-1200). Contains such oddities (mostly fakes) as the anchor of the *Santa Maria,* Toussaint L'Ouverture's watch, a sword given by Simon Bolivar to Petion, a gold plate given by President Lyndon B. Johnson to Duvalier, and Henri Cristophe's jawbone as well as the silver pistol with which he committed suicide. Other exhibits include slave bells, Indian artifacts, and a room filled with costumed dolls.

SHOPPING

Great place for window, sidewalk, and alley shopping. A flea market is held at the Maison d'Flea, near the Musee d'Arte Haitien, on Sat. mornings. Boys sell smuggled-in cartons of Kents and Marlboros along Blvd. Las Saline bordering the waterfront. **Marche de Fer (Iron Market):** Set smack-dab in the middle of Blvd. J.J. Dessalines, this brightly colored and strangely shaped red-and-green minaret-topped building, which dates from 1889, contains a wide variety of Haitian handicrafts as well as everything else under the sun. Hot and heavy bargaining is mandatory.

Oloffson Hotel

Hotel. Originally built by Pres. D.S. Sam as his palace, this Charles Addams-like structure served as the focal point for Graham Greene's classic novel *The Comedians.* To the SW of the Palais National, the Cimetiere Exterieure contains Duvalier's modest mausoleum with its eternal flame.

Cathedrale de la Sainte Trinite: Located to the N of the Champ de Mars, corner Rue Pavee and Rue Jean Marie Guillox, this Episcopal church saw the genesis of Haiti's primitive art movement. Undertaken in 1951 as an experiment under the direction of Selden Rodman and DeWitt Peters, young Haitian painters were turned loose and achieved spectacular results. Philome Obin depicts Calvary as taking place on a Haitian

art galleries: Located opposite Citibank at 92 Place Geffrard (Rue du Magasin de l'Etat), La Galerie d'Art Nader is the largest gallery in the city. Its main competitor is Issa's at 17 Rue Chile. Both have works of varying quality. Raoul Michel runs a gallery at 29 Rue Champs de Mars. Olivier's gallery is near the Hotel Oloffson. Le Centre d'Art, 56 Rue de 22 Septembre, sells paintings by major artists. Also try the shop in the Musee d'Art Haitian, the various vendors purveying their goods in front of the post office, and shops scattered through town. The most discriminating galleries are "Marassa," and Michel Mournin's in Petionville.

PRACTICALITIES

accommodation: Cheapest accommodations run from G20-25 but check to see if toilet facilities exist and are operable. St. Patrick, at G25 per room, is the best of the many hotels lining Rue du Centre. Haiti Hotel, Rue du Centre 102, charges G50 s or d (tel. 4-2665). More expensive guest house accommodation is available on the outskirts and in the suburbs of town. More upscale places include: Santos, No. 20 Rue Garoute (tel. 5-4417), Hillside, 147 Ave. Martin Luther King (tel. 5-5419), May's Villa, 28 Debussy (tel. 5-1208), Sourire Magique in

Although Haiti is the poorest country in the Americas, it has a rich tradition of folk arts. In particular, painting applies Haitian traditional folk art to a new format, one which expresses the joy, color, vitality, and sorrow inherent in the arduous life of the peasant. Although there is evidence that Haitians were heirs to a gifted artistic tradition long before WW II, it wasn't until the late 1940s that their painting gained worldwide attention. A contributing factor was the establishment of the Centre d'Art in Port-au-Prince where Haitian "primitives" were first offered for sale.

PORT-AU-PRINCE

1. Place des Heros de l'Independance (Champ de Mars)
2. Place du Marron Inconnu
3. Musee d'Art Haitien
4. Musee de Pantheon National (MUPANAH)
5. Palais National
6. Cathedrale de la Sainte Trinite
7. La Cathedrale Notre-Dame
8. l'Ancienne Cathedrale
9. Marche de Fer (Iron Market)
10. La Galerie d'Art Nader
11. Tourist Office (ONTRP)
12. Main Post Office
13. Gare du Nord (Bus station for Cap Haitien)
14. Pier for Sand Cay
15. Beau Rivage

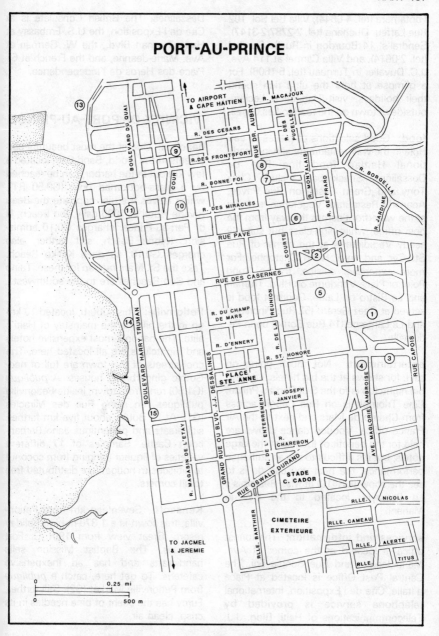

PORT-AU-PRINCE

TO AIRPORT
& CAPE HAITIEN

R. MACAJOUX

BOULEVARD DU QUAI

R. DR. AUBRY

R. DES PUCELLES

R. BORGELLA

R. DES CESARS

R. DES FRONTSFORT

R. BONNE FOI

R. DES MIRACLES

R. MONTALAIS

R. GEFFRARD

R. JARDINE

COUR

RUE PAVE

R. COURTE

RUE DES CASERNES

R. DU CHAMP
DE MARS

R. DE LA REUNION

R. D'ENNERY

R. ST. HONORE

RUE CAPOIS

PLACE
STE. ANNE

R. JOSEPH
JANVIER

AVE. MAGLOIRE AMBROISE

R. CHAREBON

BOULEVARD HARRY TRUMAN

GRAND RUE OU BLVD. J.J. DESSALINES

R. DE L' ENTERREMENT

RUE OSWALD DURAND

R. MAGASIN DE L'ETAY

STADE
C. CADOR

R. BANTHIER

TO JACMEL
& JEREMIE

CIMETIERE
EXTERIEURE

RLLE. NICOLAS

RLLE. CAMEAU

RLLE. ALERTE

RLLE. TITUS

0.25 mi

500 m

Fontamara (tel. 4-0644), Villa Bel Sol, 102 Rue Laffeur Duchene (tel. 2-2787/2-3147), Sendral's, 14 Bourdon in Ruelle Sendral (tel. 2-0614), and Villa Carmel at 114 Ave. J.C. Duvalier in Turgeau (tel. 5-1606). For a glimpse at how the ultra rich spend their holidays, visit Habitation Leclerc, outside of town on the road to Les Cayes.

food: Good selections of places to eat. Hole-in-the-wall restaurants serving traditional Haitian food line Rue de Dessalines. Snack bars include Chez Tony and Green Castle on Rue Pavee. Ananada Restaurant Vegetarien is down at the waterfront across the way from the post office, while high-class but suitably seedy Vegidiete is at the corner of Rue St. Cyr and Ave. Henri Cristophe. For more expensive cuisine, try Le Rond Point or Place Vendome on Blvd. Truman and Le Bistro on Lalue. Gourmet food is served at Chez Gerard (52 Rue Pinchinat) and La Lanterne (14 Rue Borno) up in Petionville.

entertainment: Not much going on save for shows at the big hotels. La Lambie nightclub is to the S of Port-au-Prince. Cine Triomph is on Rue Capois across from Champ de Mars and next to the Air France office. Voodoo dance shows are held for the benefit of tourists at the large hotels, but it's difficult to see an authentic performance; the best you can do is to see the show (US$10) at Max Beauvois's Le Peristyle, located to the SW in Mariani.

services and information: The tourist office is located at the corner of Ave. Marie-Jeanne and Rue Bonnie Foi. The Central Post Office is located at Place d'Italie, Cite de l'Exposition. International telephone service is provided by Telecommunications of Haiti, Bldg. J.J.

Dessalines. The British Consulate is at Cite de l'Exposition, the U.S. Embassy at Harry Truman Blvd., the W. German at Ave. Marie-Jeanne, and the French at 51 Place des Heros de l'Independence.

VICINITY OF PORT-AU-PRINCE

beaches: One of the most beautiful coral reefs in the world, Sand Cay, located a few km out in the harbor, can be reached by a glass-bottomed boat (G0.50 RT), which leaves the pier opposite the Beau Rivage Hotel at 1000 daily. Ibo Beach, N of Port-au-Prince, charges G0.10 admission. Kyona Beach, still farther, also charges G0.10, as does Kaliko Beach. Take the St. Marc *tap-tap* for these. Taino and Sun Beaches are to the southwest.

Petionville: This suburb, located 10 km up in the hills, is the mainstay of Haiti's elite. The nation's most expensive hotels and nightclubs are all located here. The cool streets of this town are full of neo-Gothic gingerbread houses. A *publique* (G1.50) runs from town; inside Petionville publiques run along Rue des Miracles (G1). At La Boule, about five km farther, sits ersatz and pretentious Jane Barbancourt Castle. Samples of 17 different varieties of liqueur (ranging from coconut to hibiscus to nougat) are distributed free to all comers.

Kenscoff: Seventeen km from Petionville, this town is a 1,370-m-high holiday resort. Great view from 19th C. Fort Jacques. The Baptist Mission sells handicrafts and has an inexpensive cafeteria. To get here, catch a *publique* from Petionville Market (G2). Still farther, Furcy has the scent of pine needles in its crisp, clean air.

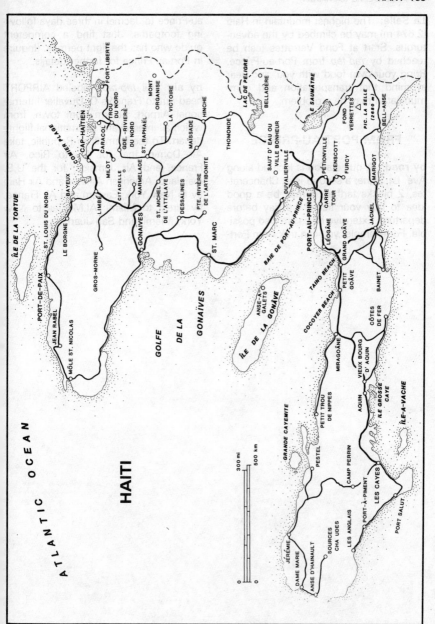

HAITI

La Selle: The highest mountain in Haiti (2,674 m) may be climbed by the adventurous. Start at Fond Verrettes (can be reached by *tap-tap* from Port-au-Prince. Bring your own food with you, and bear in mind that transportation and communicaton may be a problem.

FROM PORT-AU-PRINCE

by road: A bus station is located along Ave. La Saine; a second is at Chancerettes, 2 blocks farther. It may be a good idea to buy your ticket the day before departure. Extensive hikes are also possible. For example, you can trek from Port-au-Prince to Jacmel in three days following footpaths. Just find a competent guide who has the right permits. (Inquire in Port-au-Prince for further details.

by air: All *tap-taps* labeled AIRPORT head out to Francois C. Duvalier International Airport, 18 km from town, from which all internal and international flights depart. To the Dominican Republic, take Air Dominicana; for Puerto Rico, Air France, and Air Jamaica; for the U.S. mainland, American Airlines and Air Haiti fly to New York; Eastern and Air France, fly direct to Miami; ALM flies to New York, Miami, and San Juan.

above, clockwise: mending fish nets, Falmouth, Jamaica (Harry S. Pariser); Haitian market (Haitian National Office of Tourism); Haitian Shop (Haitian National Office of Tourism)

above: sloops in harbor, Port Antonio, Jamaica (Harry S. Pariser)
below: Presidential Palace, Port-au-Prince (Harry S. Pariser)

ONWARD TRAVEL

CAP HAITIEN

Considered the Paris of the Antilles during the 18th C., Cap Haitian, second largest city (pop. 30,000), is 258 km (160 miles) from Port-au-Prince on the N coast. This rundown but fascinating town still carries a ring of the grandeur of its rich historic past. A tourist information center is located at Rue 24, Esplanade.

history: Founded as Cap Francais by arriving buccaneers in 1670, the town grew rapidly. French emigrants from officially abandoned St. Croix added to its population. By the mid–18th C., it had become the wealthiest colonial capital in the Caribbean. Burned in 1791 and 1802 during the Haitian War of Independence, Cristophe declared the town to be his capital and ordered it rebuilt.

getting there: Takes four to 10 hours by *tap-tap* leaving from the Mahogany Market near Port-au-Prince's waterfront.

Public transportation ceases at the police checkpoint — a 15-min. walk from town. If pressed for time, it's possible to fly here or back. Avoid arriving here on Tues. and Thurs. when it's flooded with cruiseship passengers.

sights: Most notable attractions (Sans Souci and Le Citadel) are located near Milot less than an hour away. The French style neo-classic cathedral dates from 1942. The ruins of Fort Picolet are representative of French colonial military architecture. The ruins of the palace of Pauline Bonaparte (Napoleon's sister who accompanied her husband Le Clerc on his ill-fated invasion) lie on the Rue Pauline Bonaparte. Vertieres, a cactus-covered knoll outside of town, was the site of the last battle in the Haitian War of Independence. Here Dessalines beat the forces of Napoleon's veteran General Rochambeau. Vaudravil is an old planta-

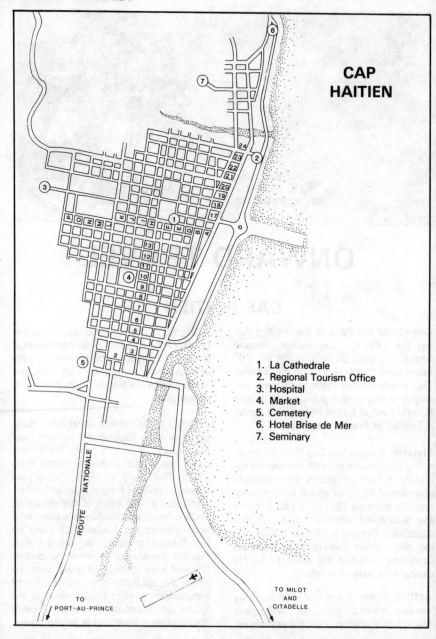

CAP HAITIEN

1. La Cathedrale
2. Regional Tourism Office
3. Hospital
4. Market
5. Cemetery
6. Hotel Brise de Mer
7. Seminary

ROUTE NATIONALE

TO
PORT-AU-PRINCE

TO MILOT
AND
CITADELLE

tion located to the east. Stone gateways on the way to Milot stand as a reminder of now vanished plantation houses. **art galleries:** These include the Galerie des Trois Visages at the end of the quay facing Hyppolite bridge and Cookoo's nest on the main shopping street.

beaches: The two with easiest access are Cormier and Coco. The former, located nine km from Le Cap, charges US$1 admission. From Cormier hire a boatman to take you to Coco Point and on to the village of Labadie where bungalows are available for about US$5. For more remote beaches try hiring fishermen on the beach near the Brise de Mer Hotel.

PRACTICALITIES

accommodations: Cheaper accommodations in town include the Bon Dieu Bon, the A a Z (located on the main square opposite the cathedral), Pension Colon (Ave. C and Rue 19-20), and Mme. Manoir's unmarked pension (Ave. E and Rue 24-25). Of the more upscale hotels, the most reasonable is the Brise de Mer which charges US$35 d.

food: Many good places to eat. Sans Raison is near the market. Sacade, corner 18 and B, is two blocks away from Universelle, a bakery and restaurant. Other restaurants are found at the corner of 6 and I, and on 11 between F and G. Fruit juices served on Ave. A between Rues 23-24.

from Cap Haitien: If you're tired from the trip up or have a tight schedule, it's possible to return by air via Turks and Caicos Airways. Flights also leave daily for the Turks and Caicos Islands, and occasionally, boats go there as well.

SANS SOUCI AND LA CITADELLE

Among the most impressive ruins in the Caribbean, if not the entire Western Hemisphere, Sans Souci and La Citadelle were the brainchild of Henri Cristophe (or King Henry I, as he had himself proclaimed), who ruled the N from 1807-20. While La Citadelle is a gigantic fortress, Sans Souci was once a palace whose lifestyle rivaled that of Versailles.

getting there: From Cap Haitien take a *publique* (G4) or *tap-tap* (G1.50) from the front of the Hotel Bon Dieu Bon Bon to the town of Milot—a ride of less than an hour. Sans Souci lies outside the town. It's about a two-hour hike (or a drive and then a short hike) to the top of La Citadelle (it's also possible to hire a guide and a horse). Be sure to bring water, food, and wear a good pair of hiking boots. Admission to Sans Souci and La Citadelle is G5.20.

Sans Souci: This palatial ruin stands outside the town of Milot. Unequalled in the West Indies, it is impressive even in decay. Although legend maintains that its design is based on Frederick the Great's Sans Souci Palace in Potsdam, in actuality the two are similar only in name. The building was clearly influenced by European palace architecture, but it's considerably smaller and lacks the fine detailing found in the former. The immense stone double staircase, which leads up to the main entrance, lends an air of grandeur to the building. Completed in 1813, the original three-story building was constructed of brick overlaid with stucco with marble floors. It was once filled with mirrors and crystal chandeliers, Gobelin tapestries, paintings, and furniture. In an early attempt at air conditioning, a simple but sophisticated cooling system carried the waters of a cool mountain stream under the marble floors. The original estate covered some 20 acres and included sentry boxes and stables. Sans Souci was the center of government, and here Cristophe, paralyzed following a stroke, committed suicide with a silver bullet. Nearby, the domed Immaculate Conception Church, built by Cristophe, was destroyed by the 1842 earthquake and restored in 1933 by President Stenio Vincent.

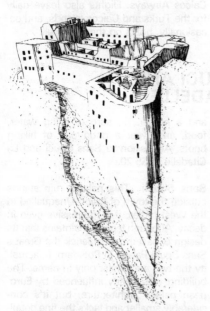

La Citadelle: *Acclaimed as the eighth wonder of the world, this defensive fortification stands unique in this hemisphere.*

the Citadelle: As a child, Henri Cristophe was familiar with (and undoubtedly deeply impressed by) Brimstone Hill on St. Kitts. Expecting the French to invade again, he ordered La Citadelle built as a refuge. Erected by thousands of workers, it served only as tomb for the multitudes who died during its construction (1804-17). As time went on, Cristophe grew more and more out of touch with reality. Once, in order to impress an emissary of George III, he ordered a platoon to walk off the upper court and fall to their deaths below. An amazing feat of hand-built human endeavor, for security reasons the German engineers who supervised its construction never set foot outside its walls again after it was completed. After Cristophe's suicide, his body was dissolved in a vat of lime in order to save it from the people's vengeance, and the uncompleted fort was left to rot in the jungle until modern times. One of the major military fortifications in the Western Hemisphere, La Citadelle is the most impressive and eeriest. Approached on foot or by horse, the structure looms out of the surrounding fog and drizzle like a phantom. Rising 40 m (130-ft.) abruptly out of the rock face, the N bastion resembles a ship's prow or a knife from the distance. Located atop a 914-m (3,000 ft.)-high mountain 20 miles from the coast, its 365 guns face the jungle. Behind them lie thousands upon thousands of never-to-be-fired cannonballs. Despite its complex innards, it is essentially a classic four-sided fort. From the top, three sides face mountains rising above mountains—some lush with vegetation, others denuded and barren—while the fourth faces a vast panorama stretching to the ocean beyond. The four gun corridors surround a spacious court containing Cristophe's tomb which is labeled "Here lies Henri Cristophe, King of Haiti. I am reborn from my ashes." Sentry boxes flank the emperor's quarters. A great chapel lies on the S bastion while a huge barracks, rising several stories, lies along the Southwest. Water was collected in huge cisterns and sugar boilers.

JACMEL

Located to the SW of Port-au-Prince, this town—with its captivating architecture—is noted for coffee, oranges, and tangerines. Although the town was nearly destroyed by fire in 1893, the houses of the coffee barons (complete with their overhanging cast-iron balconies originally brought over as ballast) still stand. Jacmel is one of the island's art centers. Selden Rodman's home, labeled "Renaissance II," has an art gallery; the marketplace is in the center of town. Nearby beaches include Cyvadier (secreted in a cove to the E of town), and Raimond-les-Baines.

accommodations: Chez Madame Luz is cheapest. Also try Guy's Guesthouse, 52 Ave. Francois Duvlier (tel. 8-3421), and Manoir Alexandra on Rue d'Orleans.

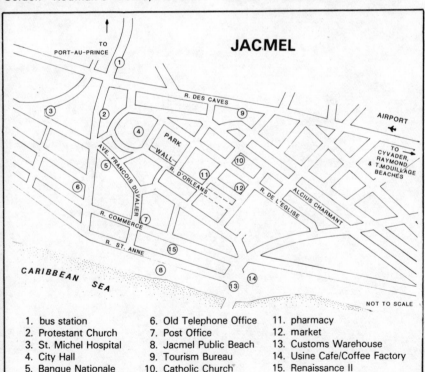

1. bus station
2. Protestant Church
3. St. Michel Hospital
4. City Hall
5. Banque Nationale
6. Old Telephone Office
7. Post Office
8. Jacmel Public Beach
9. Tourism Bureau
10. Catholic Church
11. pharmacy
12. market
13. Customs Warehouse
14. Usine Cafe/Coffee Factory
15. Renaissance II

BOOKLIST

ART, ARCHITECTURE, AND ARCHAEOLOGY

Baxter, Ivy. *The Arts of an Island.* Metuchen, New Jersey: The Scarecrow Press, Inc., 1970. A survey of Jamaican arts and art history.

Buissert, David. *Historic Architecture of the Caribbean.* London: Heinemann Educational Books, 1980.

Gosner, Pamela.*Caribbean Georgian* Washington D.C.: Three Continents Press, 1982. A beautifully illustrated guide to the "Great and Small Houses of the West Indies."

FLORA AND FAUNA

Adams, C. Dennis. *Flowering Plants of Jamaica.* Mona: University of the West Indies, 1972.

Avinoff, A. and N. Shonmatoff. *An Annotated List of Butterflies of Jamaica.* Pittsburgh: Carnegie Museum, 1946.

Bond, James.*Birds of the West Indies.* London: Collins, 1960 reprint

Eyre, Alain. *The Botanic Gardens of Jamaica.* London: Andre Deutsch, 1966.

Hawkes, Alex, and Brenda Sutton. *Wildflowers of Jamaica.* Kingston: Collins-Sangster, 1974.

Kaplan, Eugene. *A Field Guide to the Coral Reefs of the Caribbean and Florida.* Princeton, N.J.: Peterson's Guides, 1984

Lack, David. *Island Biology Illustrated by the Land Birds of Jamaica.* Berkeley and Los Angeles: University of California Press, 1976.

Romashko, Sandra. *The Shell Book of Jamaica.* Miami: Windward Publishing, 1984.

HISTORY

Ayearst, Morley. *The British West Indies.* New York: New York University Press, 1960.

Burns, Sir Alan. *History of the British West Indies.* London: George Allen and Unwin, 1954.

Cole, Hubert. *Cristophe: King of Haiti.* New York: Viking, 1967.

Cripps, L.L. *The Spanish Caribbean: From Columbus to Castro.* Cambridge, MA: Schenkman, 1979.

Davis, H.P. *Black Democracy: The Story of Haiti.* (rev. ed.) New York:Biblio and Tannen, 1967.

Diedrich, Bernard. *Papa Doc; The Truth About Haiti Today.* New York: McGraw Hill, I969.

Gingras, Jean-Pierre O. *Duvalier, Caribbean Cyclone; the History of Haiti and its Present Government.* New York, I967.

Healy, David F. *Gunboat Diplomacy in the Wilson Era: the U.S. Navy in Haiti.* Madison, Wisconsin: University of Wisconsin Press, 1976.

Hurvitz, Samuel J. and Edith F. *Jamaica: A Historical Portrait* New York: Praeger, 1971.

Knight, Franklin W. *The Caribbean.* Oxford: Oxford University Press, 1978. Thematic, anti-imperialist view of Caribbean history.

Mannix, Daniel P. and Malcolm Cooley. *Black Cargoes.* New York: Viking Press, 1982. Details the saga of the slave trade.

Nicholls, David. *From Dessalines to Duvalier.* Cambridge: Cambridge University Press, 1979. Political history of Haiti.

Phillippo, James M.*Jamaica: Its Past and Present* London: Dawson, 1969.

Williams, Eric. *From Columbus to Castro: The History of the Caribbean.* New York: Random House, 1983. Definitive history of the Caribbean by the late Prime Minister of Trinidad and Tobago.

LANGUAGE

Beckwith, Martha. *Jamaican Proverbs.* New York: Negro Universities Press, 1970.

Cassidy, Frederick G. *Jamaican Talk: Three Hundred Years of the English Language in Jamaica.* London: MacMillan Co. Ltd., 1961. Jamaican English described.

Cassidy, Frederick G. and R.B. LePage. *Dictionary of Jamaican English.* 2nd edition, Cambridge: Cambridge University Press, 1980.

LITERATURE

Bennett, Louise, et. al. *Anancy Stories and Dialect Verse.* Kingston: Pioneer Press, 1950.

Bennett, Louise. *Jamaica Labrish.* Kingston: Sangster's, 1966. More than 130 poems written in Jamaicatalk.

Greene, Graham. *The Comedians.* New York: Viking, 1981. Reprint of the classic *ton-ton macoute* novel set in Port-au-Prince.

Hearne, John. *Land of the Living.* London: Faber and Faber, 1959. By the most famous of Jamaica's novelists.

Hoffman, Leon Francois. *Essays on Haitian Literature.* Washington: Three Continents Press, 1984.

Manley, Edna. *Focus: An Anthology of Contemporary Jamaican Writing.* Mona: University College of the West Indies, 1956.

Naipaul, V.S. *Guerillas.* New York: Alfred A. Knopf, 1976. By one of the world's greatest living novelists—landscaped in Jamaica.

Patterson, Orlando. *The Children of Sisyphus.* Boston: Houghton Mifflin Co., 1965. Story of a prostitute attempting to rise in Jamaican society.

Price-Mars, Jean. *So Spoke the Uncle.* Washington, D.C.: Three Continents Press, 1984. Collection of ethnological, cultural, and literary essays by Haiti's most eminent writer.

Roumain, Jaques. *Masters of the Dew.* New York: Heinemann, 1978. A 1947 novel dealing with Haitian peasant life.

Sherlock, Phillip. *Anasi, the Spider Man, Jamaican Folk Tales.* New York: Macmillan, 1971.

Thewell, Michael. *The Harder They Come.* New York: Grove,1980. Powerful and authentic portrait of Jamaica's impoverished; inspired by the film of the same name.

MUSIC

Bergman, Billy. *Hot Sauces: Latin and Caribbean Pop.* New York: Quill, 1984.

Boot, Adrian and Goldman, Vivien. *Bob Marley: Soul Rebel, Natural Mystic.* New York: St. Martin's Press, 1982. More a pictography than a biography.

Dalrymple, Henderson. *Bob Marley: Music, Myth, and the Rastas.* London: Carib-Arawak, 1976.

Davis,Stephen. *Bob Marley.* Garden City, New York: Doubleday, 1985.

Davis, Stephen. *Reggae Bloodlines, In Search of the Music and Culture of Jamaica.* New York, Anchor Press, 1977.

Davis, Stephen and Peter Simon. *Reggae International.* New York: Alfred A. Knoph, 1982. Encyclopedic coverage of reggae history, musicians, and lifestyle on a national and international level.

Green, Jonathan. *Bob Marley and the Wailers.* London: Wise Publications, 1977.

Johnson, Howard and Jim Pines. *Reggae: Deep Roots Music.* London: Proteus, 1982.

Lewin, Olive. *Brown Gal in de Ring.* London: Oxford University Press, 1952.

White, Timothy. *Catch A Fire.* New York: Holt, Rhinehart, and Winston, 1983. Dramatized account of the life of Bob Marley. Superb discography covering Marley and everyone associated with him or the Wailers.

POLITICS AND ECONOMICS

Barry, Tom, Beth Wood, and Deb Freusch. *The Other Side of Paradise: Foreign Control in the Caribbean.* New York: Grove Press, l984. A brilliantly and thoughtfully written analysis of Caribbean economics.

Brown, Aggrey. *Colour, Class, and Politics in Jamaica.* New Jersey: Transaction Books, 1979.

Diedrich, Bernard and Al Burt. *Papa Doc: Haiti and its Dictator.* London: The Bodly Head Press, Ltd., 1970.

Lundahl, Mats. *Peasants and Poverty: A Study of Haiti.* London: Croon Helm, 1979.

Manley, Michael. *The Politics of Change: A Jamaican Testament.* London: Andre Deutsch, 1974.

Moore, O. Ernest.*Haiti: Its Stagnant Society and Shackled Economy.* New York: Exposition Press, 1972.

Rothberg, Robert I. with Christopher K. Clague. *Haiti: The Politics of Squalor.* Boston: Houghton Mifflin Co., 1971.

Weinstein, Brian and Aaron Segal. Haiti: Political Failures, Cultural Successes. New York: Praeger, 1984.

RELIGION

Barrett, Leonard. *The Rastafarians.* Boston: Beacon Press, 1977. Well written, informative account of the Rastafarian movement including an analysis of Jamaican history and related religious movements.

Clarke, John Hendrik, ed. *Marcus Garvey and the Vision of Africa.* New York: Random House, 1974.

Cronon, E.D. *Black Moses.* Madison: University of Wisconsin Press, 1966. Detailed biography of Marcus Garvey.

Deren, Maya. *Divine Horsemen.* New York: Chelsea House, 1970. A classic personal account of the Haitian religion.

Huxley, Francis. *The Invisible: Voodoo Gods in Haiti.* New York: McGraw Hill, 1970. An anthropologist recounts his experiences.

Nicholas, Tracy and Bill Sparrow. *Rastafari: A Way of Life.* New York: Anchor, 1979. Rasta history and lifestyle.

Owens, Joseph. *Dread: The Rastafarians of Jamaica.* Kingston: Sangster's, 1976. An indepth account written by a priest who taught and performed social work among the Brethren.

SOCIOLOGY AND ANTHROPOLOGY

Abrahams, Roger D. *After Africa.* New Haven: Yale University Press, 1983. Fascinating accounts of slaves and slave life in the West Indies.

Barrett, Leonard. *The Sun and the Drum.* Kingston: Sangster's, 1976. Detailed account of African influence in Jamaican culture including folk medicine, witchcraft, psychic phenomena, and language.

Brown, Aggrey. *Colour, Class, and Politics in Jamaica*. New Jersey: Transaction Books, 1979.

Clarke, Edith. *My Mother Who Fathered Me*. London: G. Allen & Unwin, 1957.

Courlander, Harold. *The Drum and The Hoe*. Berkeley and Los Angeles: University of California Press, 1960. Sweeping survey of Haitian Music, religion, and society.

Cumper, George E. *The Social Structure of Jamaica*. Mona: University College of the West Indies, 1949.

Henriques, Fernando. *Family and Colour in Jamaica*. London: Eyre and Spottiswoode, 1953.

Herskovits, Melville J. *Life in a Haitian Valley*. New York: Doubleday, Anchor Books, 1971.

Kerr, Madeline *Personality and Conflict in Jamaica*. Liverpool: Universities Press, 1952.

Kuper, Adam. *Changing Jamaica*. Kingston: Kingston Publishers, 1976. An absorbing account of social change in Jamaica.

Leyburn, James G. *The Haitian People*. (rev. ed.) New Haven: Yale University Press, 1966.

Nettleford, Rex. *Caribbean Cultural Identity: The Case of Jamaica*. Kingston: University of Jamaica, 1979.

Nettleford, Rex. *Mirror, Mirror: Identity, Race, and Protest in Jamaica*. Kingston: Collins-Sangster, 1970. Deals with the Rastafarian movement in Jamaica and the struggle for national identity.

Norris, Katrin. *Jamaica: The Search for an Identity*. London: Oxford University Press, 1962.

Price, Richard, ed. *Maroon Societies—Rebel Slave Communities in the Americas*. Garden City: Anchor Press, 1973.

Rubin, Vera and Lambros Comitas. *Ganja in Jamaica*. The Hague, Paris: Mouton & Co., 1975. A fascinating study of the effects of marijuana usage among chronic users.

Senior, Olive. *A-Z of Jamaican Heritage*. Kingston: Heinemann Educational Books, 1983. Superb, informative soft-bound encyclopedia of Jamaican history, flora, celebrations, etc.

Taylor, Frank. *Jamaica—the Welcoming Society: Myths and Reality*. Mona: University of the West Indies, 1975.

Smith, M.G., Roy Angier, and Rex Nettleford. *The Ras Tafari Movement in Kingston Jamaica*. Mona: Institute of Social and Economic Research.

Williams, K.M. *The Rastafarians*. London: Ward Lock Educational Books, 1981.

TRAVEL AND DESCRIPTION

Boot, Adrian and Thomas, Michael. *Jamaica: Babylon on a Thin Wire*. New York: Schlocken Books, 1976. Black-and-white photographic essay on Jamaica during the mid-70s.

Brand, Willem. *Impressions of Haiti*. The Hague: Mouton, 1965.

Fillingham, Paul. *Pilot's Guide to the Lesser Antilles*. New York: McGraw-Hill, 1979. Invaluable for pilots.

Floyd, Barry. *Jamaica: An Island Microcosm*. New York: St. Martin's Press, 1979. Concise description of island realities.

Hart, Jeremy C. and William T. Stone. *A Cruising Guide to the Caribbean and the Bahamas*. New York: Dodd, Mead and Company, 1982. Description of planning and plying for yachties. Includes nautical maps.

Morrison, Samuel E. *The Caribbean as Columbus Saw It.* Boston: Little and Co.: 1964. Photographs and text by a leading American historian.

Naipaul, V.S. *The Middle Passage: The Caribbean Revisited.* New York: MacMillan, 1963. Another view of the West Indies by a Trinidad native.

Radcliffe, Virginia. *The Caribbean Heritage.* New York: Walker & Co., 1976.

Rodman, Selden. *The Caribbean.* New York: Hawthorn & Co., 1968. Traveler's description of Haiti by the leading historian, poet, and art critic.

Rodman, Selden. *Haiti: The Black Republic.* Greenwich, Ct.: Devin-Adair, 1961.

Wright, Philip and Paul F. White. *Exploring Jamaica: A Guide for Motorists.* New York: W.W. Norton & Co., Inc. 1969. Outdated, but still of great value.

GLOSSARY

ackee—fruit introduced from West Africa which is boiled and cooked together with saltfish or salt pork. National fruit of Jamaica.

aloe—medicinal plant, bitter to the taste, which originated in Southern Africa. Commonly known in Jamaica as *sinkle bible.*

Anancy—the Jamaican equivalent of America's Brer Rabbit tales. Originated with the Ghanain Asante tribe; Anancy is usually portrayed as a spider.

Arawaks—Indians who originated in the Orinoco region of South America. Supplanting earlier arrivals in the Caribbean like the Ciboneys, they were exterminated by the Spanish, and by the war-like Caribs in the southern islands.

balm—system of natural medicine. Commonly practiced in Jamaica by balmists who mintain their own balmyard; treatment normally involves the use of herbs ("bush") in the form of baths and teas.

bammy—deep-fried casava bread which originated with the Arawaks; commonly served at Jamaican roadside stands along with fried fish.

bankra—Jamaican basket; name is derived from the Twi language of Ghana *(bonkara).*

bauhnia—flowering plant or bush, usually with pink and lavender blossoms, indigenous to the Caribbean. A popular ornamental plant.

bauxite—ore from which aluminum is made. Jamaica at one time was the world's leading producer.

bissy—the cola nut, of African origin; a stimulant, it is used as a poison antidote, as medicine, and to make the drink of the same name.

bladderwort—a floating, insect-eating plant; commonly found on the Black River morass in Jamaica.

bocor—Haitian Voodoo sorcerer

bomboche—secular holiday (birthday, wedding, etc.) held in Haiti.

bulla—Jamaican traditional cake; small, flat, and round; made with flour, molasses, and soda.

cacoon—vine, found in many parts of tropical America including Jamaica. Its bean pods may extend to five feet in length.

calabash—small tree native to the Caribbean whose fruit, a gourd, has multiple uses when dried.

cassava — a staple crop indigenous to the Americas. Bitter and sweet are the two varieties. Bitter must be grated, washed, and baked in order to remove the poisonous prussic acid. Jamaican bammy is made from the bitter variety as is casareep, a preservative which is the foundation of West Indian pepperpot stew.

cays—Arawak-originated name which refers to islets in the Caribbean.

Carib—name of Indian tribe who colonized the islands of the Caribbean, giving the region its name.

coco—Jamaican name for *tannia* and *yautia.* A staple food in the Caribbean, this tuber was originally imported from Polynesia (where it is known as taro) by the Portuguese.

combite (coumbite)—cooperative work effort performed to the beat of Haitian drums.

coney—land mammal indigenous to the Caribbean. This small brown rodent, a favorite food ofthe Arawaks, has become nearly extinct owing to the mongoose and modernization.

conch—large, edible mollusk usually pounded into salads or chowders.

coratoe—also known as karato, maypole, and the century plant. Flowers only once in its lifetime before it dies.

djon-djon—miniature Haitian mushrooms considered a delicacy.

doctor bird—known to the Arawaks as God bird, it was believed to be the reincarnation of a dead soul and to have magical properties.

dread or dreadlocks—term connoting a Rastafarian or one sporting a Rastafarian hair style.

duppy—ghost or spirit of the dead which is feared throughout the Caribbean. Derives from the African religious belief that a man has two souls: one ascends to heaven while the other stays around for a while or permanently. May be harnessed for good or evil through *obeah*. Some plants and birds are also associated with duppies.

EP—Europeon Plan.

escovitch—Spanish and Portugese method of marinating seafood which has been transfused into Jamaican cuisine.

galliwasp—Jamaican lizard which is incorrectly believed to be poisonous.

ganja—Jamaican name for marijuana which was introduced into Jamaica by indentured workers from India.

guava—indigenous Caribbean fruit, extremely rich in vitamin C, which is eaten raw or used in making jelly.

guinep—small green fruit found iun Jamaica and Surinam.

gungo peas—mottled green and brown peas which are a favorite Jamaican food. Commonly found in rice and peas or soup, and also known as pidgeon or congo peas.

higgler—Jamaican marketeers or vendors. Traditionally female, they form the backbone of Jamaica's internal marketing system. Once the intermediary between farmer and housewife, they now board planes for Miami and Port-au-Prince and return with goods for sale.

houngan—male Haitian Voodoo priest.

hounsi—male Voodoo initiate.

hussay—traditional processional festival still celebrated by Jamaica's East Indian Muslim community.

Irish moss—Jamaican health food drink made using a seaweed extract.

jackass corn—Jamaican biscuit made from coconut and sugar.

jackfruit—yellow fleshy fruit which grows inside enormous pods extending from the trunk of the tree of the same name; seeds may be roasted or boiled and eaten.

jerk pork—famous Jamaican-style of preparation originated by the Maroons and in common use throughout the island. Pimento wood gives it its special flavor. Also used to prepare chicken and fish.

jew plum—huge, greenish yellow plum which is stewed to make a Jamaican dessert—orignated in the South Pacific.

John Crow—a scavenger bird (a type of buzzard) commonly seen in Jamaica.

Jonkonnu—festivities dating from the plantation era in which bands of masqueraders, dressed with horse or cow heads or as kings, queens, or devils parade through the streets.

khus khus—grass used in making Jamaican perfume and toilet water.

Kumina (Cumina)—an ancester worship cult of Bantu origin. Very popular in Jamaica.

lignum vitae—native to tropical America. One of the most useful trees in the world. Its blue flower is the national flower of Jamaica.

loa—Voodoo god

love bush—orange colored parasitic vine, found on Jamaica, St. John, and other Caribbean islands. Resembles nothing so much as the contents of a can of Franco-American spaghetti.

MAP—Modified American Plan; accommodation including breakfast and dinner.

mahoe—indigenous Caribbean tree; national flower of Jamaica.

mambo—female Voodoo priestess.

manatee—the sea cow, mistaken by Columbus for mermaids. An endangered species, less than 14,000 exist in the world.

Maroons—members of runaway slave communities in the Americas. Largest group of Maroons are in Jamaica.

massif—mountain mass on Haiti.

mento—Jamaican folk music, forerunner of calypso and reggae, now rarely performed.

myal—Caribbean white magic which became a religious cult and then faded. It included herbal medicine and the capture and control of duppies (ghosts) for positive purposes. Many of its features have been incorporated into Kumina and other revival religions.

negritude—pride in black African heritage esposued by Haitian elite under Francois Duvalier

obeah—Caribbean black magic imported from Africa. In Jamaica "bushdoctor" (herbal medicine) and "science" (based on the books of American black magician De Laurence) are practiced illegally.

ortanique—cross between a tangerine and an orange. A Jamaican fruit, its name is a combination of orange, tangerine, and unique.

otaheite apple—crimson fruit, shaped like a pear. Originated in Polynesia.

Pantomime—Jamaican annual theatrical event produced by the Little Theater Movement.

patty—Jamaican-style fast food consisting of pastry dough with spicy ground filling.

pimento—internationally known as allspice because it is said to combine the flavors of nutmeg, clove, cinnamon, and pepper. Highest quality grown in jamaica.

rice and peas—dish made from rice cooked with beans, seasoning, and coconut milk.

sea grape—West Indian tree commonly found along beaches which produces green, fleshy, inedible grapes.

sinsemilla—term used to describe the highest grade of Jamaican ganja (marijuana).

sorrel—originally from the Sudan, the red stems and chalices of this bushy shrub are brewed by Jamaicans to make a popular Christmas drink.

stamp and go—fried and seasoned codfish fritters found at roadside stands in Jamaica.

star apple—native of the Greater Antilles, the round fruit of this tree is always green or purple when ripe. It reveals a star-shaped pattern when sliced in the center.

tamarind—large tree producing segmented pods, brown in color and sour in taste, which are a popular Jamaican fruit.

tap-taps—colorfully painted buses (small covered pickup trucks with board seats) found in urban areas of Haiti.

ton-ton macoutes—the bagmen employed by Francois Duvalier.

ugli—warty and irregular citrus fruit, larger than a grapefruit. Jamaican hybrid—a cross between a tangerine and a grapefruit.

Voodoo—Haitian religious system whch consists of a reblending of West African religions and Catholicism.

woman's tongue—Asian plant whose name comes from its long seed pods; dry when brown, they flutter and rattle in the breeze, constantly making noise.

yabba—large earthenware bowl still made in Jamaica. Of African origin, it has strong European influences in its design.

yampi—the only species of yam indigenous to Jamaica.

zemi—idol in which the personal spirit of each Arawak or Taino Indian lived. Usually carved from stone.

INDEX

KEY JA = Jamaica; HA = Haiti *"i"* = illustration and caption; "c" = chart; *"m"* = map.

ABOUT THE AUTHOR

Harry S. Pariser was born in Pittsburgh and grew up in a small town in Pennsylvania. After graduating from Boston University with a B.S. in Public Communications in 1975, Harry hitched and camped his way through Europe, traveled down the Nile by steamer, and by train through Sudan. After visiting Uganda, Rwanda, and Tanzania, he traveled by passenger ship from Mombasa to Bombay, and then on through South and Southeast Asia before settling down in Kyoto, Japan, where he studied Japanese and ceramics while supporting himself by teaching English to everyone from tiny tots to Buddhist priests. Using Japan as a base, he returned to other parts of Asia: trekking to the vicinity of Mt. Everest in Nepal, taking tramp steamers to remote Indonesian islands like Adonara, Timor, Sulawesi, and Ternate, and visiting rural areas in China. Returning to the United States in 1984 from Kanazawa, Japan, via the Caribbean (where he researched this book), he now lives in the Haight area of San Francisco where he reviews music concerts, cooks his own version of Asian food, draws etchings, and listens to jazz music.

Harry slides down the upper slopes of the summit of Gunung Lokon in Minahasa Province, North Sulawesi, Indonesia.

OTHER
MOON PUBLICATIONS
GUIDES

Indonesia Handbook 3rd. edition
by Bill Dalton

Not only is *Indonesia Handbook* the most complete and contemporary guide to Indonesia yet prepared, it is a sensitive analysis and description of one of the world's most fascinating human and geographical environments. It is a travel encyclopedia which scans, island by island, Indonesia's history, ethnology, art forms, geography, flora and fauna—while making clear how the traveler can move around, eat, sleep and generally enjoy an utterly unique travel experience in this loveliest of archipeligos. The London Times called *Indonesia Handbook* "one of the best practical guides ever written about any country." 137 illustrations and b/w photos, 123 maps, appendicies, booklist, glossary, index. 602 pages.

Code MN01   **$12.95**

South Pacific Handbook 3rd. edition
by David Stanley

Here is paradise explored, photographed and mapped—the first original, comprehensive guide to the history, geography, climate, cultures, and customs of the 19 territories in the South Pacific. Experience awesome Bora Bora by rented bicycle; scale Tahiti's second highest peak; walk down a splendidly isolated, endless talcum beach in New Caledonia's Loyalty Islands; drink *kava* with villagers in Fiji's rugged·interior; backpack through jungles in Vanuatu to meet the "Hidden People"; marvel at the gaping limestone chasms of Niue; trek along Bloody Ridge in the Solomons where the Pacific War changed course; hitch rides on cruising yachts; live the life of a beachcomber in Tonga; witness the weaving of a "fine mat" under a Samoan *fale*; go swimming with free sea lions in the Galapagos; dive onto coral gardens thick with brilliant fish; see atoll life unchanged in Tokelau or Tuvalu; dance the exciting Polynesian dances of the Cooks. No other travel book covers such a phenomenal expanse of the earth's surface. 588 Smyth-sewn pages, 121 illustrations, 195 black and white photos, 12 color pages, 138 maps, 35 charts, booklist, glossary, index. 588 pages

Code MN03   **$13.95**

Japan Handbook
by J.D. Bisignani

Packed with practical money-saving tips on travel, food and accommodation, this book dispels the myth that Japan is "too expensive" for the budget-minded traveler. The theme throughout is "do it like the Japanese," to get the most for your time and money. From Okinawa through the entire island chain to Rishiri Island in the extreme north, *Japan Handbook* is essentially a cultural and anthropological manual on every facet of Japanese life. 35 color photos, 200 b/w photos, 92 illustrations, 29 charts, 112 maps and town plans, an appendix on the Japanese language, booklist, glossary, index. 504 pages.

Code   MN05   **$12.95**

Guide to Catalina Island
by Chicki Mallan

Whether they come by yacht, ferry, or airplane, visitors to Santa Catalina will find this the most complete guide to California's most unique island. *Guide to Catalina Island* provides essential travel information, including complete details on hotels, restaurants, camping facilities, bike and boat rentals; it covers as well boat moorings and skindiving locales, making it a must for marine enthusiasts. Everyone, however, will benefit from *Guide to Catalina's* other features—historical background, natural history, hiking trail guides, general travel and recreation tips. 4 color pages, photos and illustrations, index, 142 pages.

Code   MN09   **$5.95**

Backpacking: A Hedonist's Guide
by Rick Greenspan and Hal Kahn

This humorous, informative, handsomely illustrated how-to guide will convince even the most confirmed naturophobe that it's safe, easy, and enjoyable to leave the smoggy security of city life behind. *Backpacking: A Hedonist's Guide* covers all the backpacking basics—equipment, packing, maps, trails—but it places special emphasis on how to prepare such surprising culinary wonders as trout quiche, sourdough bread, chocolate cake, even pizza, over the fragrant coals of a wilderness campfire. This book won't catch trout or bake cake but it will, however, provide the initial inspiration, practical instruction, and cut the time, cost, and hard-knocks of learning. 90 illustrations, annotated booklist, index, 199 pages.

Code   MN23   **$7.95**

Alaska-Yukon Handbook
A Gypsy Guide to the Inside Passage and Beyond
by David Stanley

Embark from exciting cities such as Seattle, Vancouver, and Victoria, and sail to Alaska on the legendary Inside Passage. Tour the great wilderness ranges and wildlife parks of the North. Backpack across tundra to snowcapped peaks; stand high above the largest glaciers on earth; run mighty rivers. See nature as it once was everywhere. Travel by regular passenger ferry, bus, and train, or just stick out your thumb and go. Sleep in campgrounds, youth hostels, and small hotels tourists usually miss. Dine in unpretentious local eating places or just toss out your line and pull in a salmon. In addition to thousands of specific tips on Alaska and Yukon, this handbook includes detailed coverage of Washington and British Columbia. *Alaska-Yukon Handbook* is the only travel guide which brings this whole spectacular region within reach of everyone. 37 color photos, 76 b/w photos, 86 illustrations, 70 maps, booklist, glossary, index, 230 pages.

Code MN07   **$7.95**

Micronesia Handbook
by David Stanley

Apart from atomic blasts at Bikini and Enewetak in the late 40s and early 50s, the vast Pacific area between Hawaii and the Philippines has received little attention. For the first time, *Micronesia Handbook* cuts across the plastic path of packaged tourism and guides you on a real Pacific adventure uniquely your own. Its 210 packed pages cover the seven North Pacific territories in detail. All this, plus 35 maps, charts, color pages, photos, drawings, index. 210 pages.

Code MN19   **$7.95**

Finding Fiji
by David Stanley

Fiji, everyone's favorite South Pacific country, is now easily accessible either as a stopover or a whole Pacific experience in itself. No visis or vaccinations are required! Enjoy picture-window panoramas as you travel from exciting island resorts where Australians meet Americans halfway, to remote interior valleys where you can backpack from village to village. You'll fall immediately in love with Fiji's friendly, exuberant people. *Finding Fiji* covers it all—the amazing variety of land and seascapes, customs and climates, sightseeing attractions, hikes, beaches, and how to board a copra boat to the outer islands. *Finding Fiji* is packed with practical tips, everything you need to know in one portable volume. 20 color photos, 78 illustrations, 26 maps, 3 charts, vocabulary, subject and place name index, 127 pages.

Code MN17   **$6.95**

MAPS

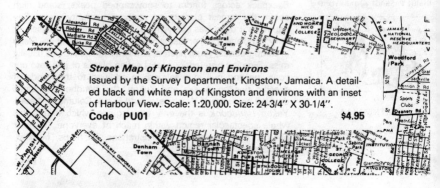

Street Map of Kingston and Environs
Issued by the Survey Department, Kingston, Jamaica. A detailed black and white map of Kingston and environs with an inset of Harbour View. Scale: 1:20,000. Size: 24-3/4" X 30-1/4".
Code PU01 $4.95

Jamaica by Hildebrand Maps
Hildebrand Maps produces a new line of sturdily-packaged maps designed especially for the traveler. This beautiful full-color map clearly presents Jamaica's topography, roads, towns and cities. The map is entirely up-to-date and thoroughly researched. Included on the map are facts and information of special interest to the traveler—climate, points-of-interest, currency, transportation, postal and telephone information, as well as detailed street maps of important areas. Scale: 1:400,000. Folded.
Code HD06 $5.95

West Indies and the Caribbean by Bartholomew
Bartholomew World Travel Maps are an internationally aclaimed series of detailed topographic maps, ideal for travel use. Using layer coloring to show relief, this fine, large format, easy-to-read map of the Caribbean clearly portrays all major and well-traveled sideroads, railways, and airports. Cities are graded by population where possible and items of special interest such as major antiquities and local landscape types are emphasized. The map is both political and physical in style and all detail is kept up-to-date. Size: 30" X 40". Folded size: 6" X 10".
Code BA40 $6.95

OF RELATED INTEREST

The Tropical Traveller
by John Hatt

Compiled in this completely revised and updated new edition
are over a thousand tips, covering every aspect of tropical
travel—from travellers' cheques to salt tablets, from bribery to
mugging, from mosquito bites to shark attack. Whether you are
a sunbather, tourist, backpacker or explorer, you'll be sure
to benefit from this amusing and reassuring reference book.
"Helpful, accurate and funny" wrote the *International Herald
Tribune.* Highly readable. 67 pages.

Code HI43 $8.95

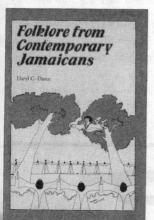

Folklore From Comtemporary Jamaicans
by Daryl C. Dance

The first comprehensive anthology of the rich folklore of
Jamaica offers a fascinating and informative introduction to
contemporary Jamaican life and culture. 20 photographs, 11
original drawings, 2 maps. Hardcover. 272 pages

Code UT01 $23.95

Exploring Tropical Isles and Seas: An Introduction for the Traveler and Amateur Naturalist
by Frederic Martini

With this entertaining and engrossing book , you'll learn about
life on and around tropical isles—the climate, precipitation, and
ocean currents—plus find handy information on the population,
language, currency, and size of the islands. You'll also discover
how natural forces like volcanos and erosion are constantly
creating, shaping. and destroying islands and entire island
groups. *Exploring Tropical Isles and Seas* even comes complete
with detailed coverage of potential medical problems and pre-
cautions, including advice on how to treat coral cuts, stings,
rashes, infections, and sunburn. This factbook will enhance
your traveling experience a thousandfold. Covers the Hawaiian
Is., Samoa, Galapagos, Tonga, Fiji, Guam, Palau, Barbados,
Martinique, Jamaica, Puerto Rico, the Bahamas, and the Virgin
Islands.

Code PH70 $15.95

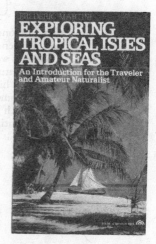

IMPORTANT ORDERING INFORMATION

1. *prices:* Due to foreign exchange fluctuations and the changing terms of our distributers, all prices for books and maps on these ad pages are subject to change without notice.

2. *domestic orders:* For bookrate (3-4 weeks delivery), send $1.25 for first book and $.50 for each additional book. For UPS or USPS 1st class (3-7 days delivery), send $3.00 for first book and $.50 for each additional book. For UPS 2nd Day Air, call for a quote.

3. *foreign orders:* All orders which originate outside the U.S.A. **must** be paid for with either an International Money Order or a check in U.S. currency drawn on a major U.S. bank based in the U.S.A. For International Surface Bookrate (3-12 weeks delivery), send U.S.$2.00 for the first book and U.S.$1.00 for each additional book. If you'd like your book(s) sent Printed Matter Air-mail, write us for a quote before sending money.

4. *Visa and Mastercharge payments:* Minimum order US$15.00. Telephone orders are accepted. Call (916) 345-5473 or 345-5413.

5. *noncompliance:* Any orders received which do not comply with any of the above conditions will result in a delay in fulfilling your order or the return of your order and/or payment intact.

Moon Belts

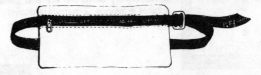

A new concept in money belts. Made from highly durable, water repellent polyester cotton blend fabric for maximum all-weather comfort. The 3.75x8 inch pouch is worn around the waist concealed inside your clothes. Many thoughtful features: One inch wide nylon webbing, heavy duty zipper, and 1 inch wide high test plastic slide for easy adjustability. The field-tested Moon Belt comes with extra long webbing; cut to your size, then simply seal end with lighted match. Accommodates Travelers Checks, passport, cash. Essential for the traveler. Only $5.95.

NOTES

ORDER FORM
(See important ordering information previous page)

Name _____

Address_____

City _____

State or Country_____Zip_____

Quantity	Full Book or Map Title	Code	Price

California Residents please add 6 percent Sales Tax

Domestic Shipping Charges for 1st item: $1.25

($.50 for each additional item)

Additional charges for International or UPS postage

TOTAL ENCLOSED

Make checks payable to:

MOON PUBLICATIONS   P.O. BOX 1696   CHICO   CALIFORNIA   95927-1696   USA

WE ACCEPT VISA AND MASTERCHARGE!

Please send written order with your Visa or Mastercharge number and expiry date clearly written

CHECK/MONEYORDER ENCLOSED FOR $ _____

CARD NO.   ☐ VISA   ☐ MASTERCHARGE   BANK NO.

☐☐☐☐☐☐☐☐☐☐☐☐☐☐☐☐☐☐☐☐   ☐☐☐☐

SIGNATURE_____ EXPIRATION DATE_____

THANK YOU FOR YOUR ORDER